Klaus Hinz, Petra Schmidt

People Around You

An Introductory Course:
English Sek. II

Enriched Version

Best.-Nr. 040007 1

Schöningh Verlag

Dr. Klaus Hinz, Fachbereichsleiter Fremdsprachen (NRW-Lehrerfortbildungsinstitut)

Petra Schmidt, Studiendirektorin, Fachleiterin für Englisch

Acknowledgements

Illustrations
p. 31: © laenderpress/PRI; p. 34: © RSE/laenderpress, Düsseldorf; p. 36: © William Borden, Bemidji, USA; p. 37: Günter Schlottmann, Delbrück; p. 38: Scholastic Update, Vol. 121, No. 14, March 24, 1989, p. 13; p. 39: Kevin Lyles: Vietnam: US Uniformen der Bodentruppen. Düsseldorf: Barett Verlag 1992, p. 7, © 1992 by Windrow & Greene; p. 49: Peace tales. World folktales to talk about. By Margaret Read MacDonald. Linnet Books 1992; p. 54: Guest Quick Guide, August/September 1993, p. 12; p. 59: © AKG, Berlin; p. 60: Archiv für Kunst und Geschichte, Berlin; p. 61: Guest Quick Guide, August/September 1993, p. 69
Further Illustrations: Authors of PEOPLE AROUND YOU - ENRICHED VERSION

Texts
Locker 160 by Lee Busselman. Sun & Shadow 1971, p. 96. © 1971 by Scholastic Inc.
The Big Race by Toby Sweet. W.H. Smith: Young Words. Award-winning entries from the 1985 W.H. Smith Young Writers' Competition. London 1986. © Pan Macmillan Children's Books, London
Manhood by John Wain. Michael Knight: Keep in Touch. Hemel Hempstead: Prentice Hall, p. 36 © Prentice Hall, Hemel Hempstead
Jumping by William Borden. © William Borden, Rt. 6, Box 284, Bemidji, MN 56601, USA
The Split Decision by William Moseley. Norman Bert: One-Act Plays of Acting Students. Colorado Springs: Meriwether Publishing LTD 1987, pp. 45–53. 1987. © William Moseley, 102 Highview Drive, Cocoa, Florida 32922, USA. Permission of the author must be obtaines for any public performance of this play.
The Ballad of the Green Berets by Barry Sadler and Robin Moore. © by EMI Music Publishing Germany GmbH, Hamburg
The Children by William Soutar. Poems of our time. Ed. by R. Church, M. Bozman, E. Sitwell. London: Everyman's Library 1945.
Grass by Carl Sandburg. Richard Ellman: The New York Oxford Book of American Verse. New York, pp. 423–424.
O Great Spirit by Tom Whitecloud. A Return of the Indian Spirit. Ed. by Winston Brown. 1991, p. 61.
Imagine by John Lennon. © NORDTON MUSIKVERLAG, GMBH, Berlin (Budde)
Peace by Robert Muller. © Robert Muller, Ap. 3, 150 Draper Lane, Dobbs Ferry, New York, N.Y. 10522, USA
Reprinted courtesy of The Boston Globe: *"In Duxbury High test, subject is alcohol use,"* by Bob Hohler, Oct. 19, 1993.

Gedruckt auf umweltfreundlichem, chlorfrei gebleichtem Papier.

Website
www.schoeningh.de

E-Mail
info@schoeningh.de

Alle deutschsprachigen Teile dieses Werks folgen der reformierten Rechtschreibung und Zeichensetzung.

Illustrationen: Christiane Zay, Bielefeld

Druck: westermann druck GmbH, Braunschweig

Druck 9 8 7 6 Jahr 05 04 03 02

ISBN 3-14-040007-1

Table of Contents

	Vorwort	4
Unit 1: Doing the Right Thing – The Short Story	Getting into the Unit	5
	Locker 160 (Lee Busselman)	7
	The Big Race (Toby Sweet)	10
	Manhood (John Wain)	15
	Project	26
Unit 2: Love is ... - The Drama	Getting into the Unit	27
	Jumping (William Borden)	28
	An Interview with William Borden	35
	Project	37
Unit 3: Paths to Peace - Poetry	Getting into the Unit	38
	The Ballad of the Green Berets (Barry Sadler, Robin Moore)	39
	The Children (William Soutar)	41
	Grass (Carl Sandburg)	43
	O Great Spirit (Tom Whitecloud)	45
	Imagine (John Lennon)	46
	Be Peaceful ... (Robert Muller)	48
	Project	49
Unit 4: Boston: Today and Yesterday – Non-fictional Texts	Getting into the Unit	50
	Boston's Layout	52
	Aspects of Life in Boston	54
	Boston: the Cradle of the United States	58
	Project	62
Unit 5: Why do people say what they say the way they say it? – Language	Getting into the Unit	63
	Registers	64
Appendix 1:	**Writer's Workshop**	
	Note-taking	67
	Writing a paragraph	68
	Summary-writing	69
	Characterization	71
	Giving opinions	73
	Story-telling	75
	Letter-writing	76
	Diary-writing	77
	Writing a newspaper article	78
	Comparing texts	79
Appendix 2:	**Glossary of Terms for Text Analysis**	81
Appendix 3:	**Vocabulary for Text Analysis and Text Production**	85
Appendix 4:	**Grammar Exercises**	89

Vorwort

Das vorliegende Arbeitsbuch richtet sich an Schülerinnen und Schüler der beginnenden Sekundarstufe II und ist als Einführung in oberstufengemäße Arbeitsverfahren im Fach Englisch unter Berücksichtigung der Richtlinien für die Sekundarstufe II konzipiert.

Im Einzelnen werden folgende Ziele verfolgt:

- Vorstellung verschiedener Textsorten
- Einführung in Methoden der inhaltlichen Analyse und Interpretation fiktionaler und nicht-fiktionaler Texte
- Einführung in Verfahren der Sprach- und Stilanalyse im Rahmen der Textarbeit
- Anleitung zur Gestaltung der persönlichen Stellungnahme
- systematische prozessorientierte Erweiterung der schriftsprachlichen Kompetenz

Die Texte sind unter dem Gesichtspunkt ihrer Zugehörigkeit zu einem auf das betreffende Kapitel bezogenen Thema in kürzeren, nach Textsorten gegliederten *Units* zusammengefasst.

Die methodische Verfahrensweise lehnt sich an neuere lernpsychologische und methodische Erkenntnisse an. Das besondere Merkmal liegt in der Bearbeitung der Texte anhand von *pre-reading-, while-reading-* und *post-reading-*Aufgaben.
Die dem Text vorgeschaltete *pre-reading*-Aufgabe führt zum Text, Thema oder Problem hin und dient auch als Leseanreiz.
Das besondere Merkmal des Layouts ist die Unterteilung der Seite in eine Textspalte und eine Funktionsspalte am rechten Rand mit *while-reading*-Aufgaben. Die mit Pfeilen versehenen Aufgaben begleiten den Lesevorgang und erleichtern das Textverständnis. Ein nach oben gerichteter Pfeil zeigt an, dass sich die Aufgabe auf den gerade gelesenen Textteil bezieht, eine mit einem nach innen weisenden Pfeil versehene Aufgabe bezieht sich auf die betreffende Textstelle und ein nach unten gerichteter Pfeil verknüpft die Aufgabe mit dem nachfolgenden Text als so genannte Beobachtungsanleitung. Mit Hilfe der *while-reading*-Aufgaben wird das Verständnis der Oberflächenstruktur des Textes im Rahmen eines *"guided reading"* sichergestellt.
Die sich an den Text anschließenden *post-reading*-Aufgaben sind vertiefender Art und beziehen sich auf Interpretation, Stilanalysen, Schreibaufgaben etc.

Unit 1 Doing the Right Thing

Getting into the Unit

Do you think the people's behaviour in these situations is right or wrong? Give reasons for your ideas.

One afternoon, Frank and Mike went to the big local hifi-shop. Frank had told Mike about the fantastic new personal CD-player he had seen there. When they arrived at the right shelf there was no shop assistant to be seen. Suddenly Frank unpacked one of the CD-players, took out an old plastic carrier bag and put the CD-player in. "Come on, Mike", he said, "let's get out of here." The boys managed to slip past the check-out while someone else was paying.

Janet had always been good at maths. During a test she was sitting behind her best friend Clarisse who was not as good at maths as Janet. Clarisse passed Janet a slip of paper asking for some help with a difficult problem. But Janet was so busy doing the test herself that she refused to help Clarisse.

One day Mr Dawson discovered that one of his favourite books had gone. He remembered that he had lent it to his old friend, Mr Philips. The next day he phoned his friend to ask him if he still needed the book. But Mr Philips said that he had returned it a long time ago. The two men quarrelled, both convinced that they were right. Weeks later Mr Dawson found the lost book in a pile of old books he had wanted to give away. Feeling very sorry, he tried to apologise to Mr Philips. But his old friend was so hurt that he did not want to talk to Mr Dawson again.

The Short Story

A short story is a short fictional text[1]. It deals with one or two main characters and one main event or conflict. The elements of a short story are characters (persons in a fictional text), setting (the place and time at which the events take place), theme (central idea), and plot (series of events).

Before you read the short story "Locker 160":

Lockers in a school

A locker plays an important part in the story.

- It was clear that Miriam had seen the note.
- Julie and I arrived at school early.
- It was my idea, I guess, in the first place.
- The tardy bell[2] rang, but Miriam still hadn't come.
- As I came near locker 160, I looked around to make sure nobody was watching.

The following sentences are from *Locker 160* but they have been mixed up. Can you put them in the right order and say what the story could be about?

[1]**fictional text** (e.g. a story, a drama or a poem are fictional texts) – [2]**tardy bell** (AE) a signal that class is about to begin

Locker 160 Lee Busselman

It was my idea, I guess, in the first place. "Let's put a hate note in someone's locker," I said to Julie, half as a joke. We were waiting for biology class to begin. She smiled and raised her eyebrows. "Another one of your great ideas, Karen? Whose locker do you suggest we put it in?"

✓ What is Karen's idea?

I glanced around the room. "Oh - Miriam." It wasn't that we really – I mean *really* – hated Miriam. That is, we both said "Good morning" to her and "See you tomorrow." But she was just – well, different.

✓ Why does she choose Miriam as her victim?

In spite of the fact that she was pretty, with long, black hair and a graceful figure, she wasn't popular. Miriam always kept to herself. Besides that, she wrote poetry – that weird[1], free verse kind that nobody can understand. That was how it began.

The next morning, Julie and I arrived at school early. We planned to write a note and put it in Miriam's locker, number 160. "What should we say?" I asked. I held my pencil over a piece of notebook paper.

"Something simple. How about 'You stink'?"

I printed the message in large, untidy letters. "There," I said, handling the paper to Julie.

"I don't want it. You take it." She pushed the note back. "I'm scared[2]."

I didn't want to, but I took the paper. My hands trembled as I walked down the hallway. I heard the loud clack of my footsteps on the linoleum. As I came near locker 160, I looked around to make sure nobody was watching. There was only Julie, peeking[3] around the corner of the hall.

Karen and Julie

Miriam

I opened Miriam's locker. The books were neatly piled[4] on the metal shelf. A notebook with "Miriam Laker" written on it was beside them.

I placed our note on her notebook, where she would be sure to see it. I closed the locker door und walked away, with a pleasant feeling of relief[5]. We stayed in the hall almost 15 minutes, waiting for Miriam to arrive. Then Julie nudged[6] me and whispered, "Here she comes."

Miriam went directly to her locker.

"Look," Julie whispered. "Look at her face."

We burst out laughing. It was clear that Miriam had seen the note. Her face looked as if she had been hit with a wet dish rag. Julie and I fled, giggling[7], to the rest room.

< What might the girls think at this moment?

After that it was easy.

[1]**weird** [wɪəd] strange, unnatural - [2]**scared** very afraid - [3]**to peek** to look - [4]**to pile** to put a lot of things on top of one another - [5]**relief** taking away pain or worry - [6]**to nudge** to touch or push gently - [7]**to giggle** to laugh in a silly way

The next day, we arranged an open plastic bag of marbles[1] in Miriam's locker. When the hundreds of marbles went bouncing and clattering down the hallway, I wonder how she explained it to the principal[2]. He was standing nearby when it happened.

After that, Julie got the idea of making a voodoo[3] doll of Miriam. I must say we did an excellent job. We used a large carrot for the body, and a small onion with black yarn for the head.

After we drew the face on in ink, we stuck a huge hat pin through the onion. Then we hung a tiny sign on the doll that said "Miriam". I thought it looked rather cute[4] on the shelf of Miriam's locker.

We reached a new height the next day. Julie had a petition[5] to change the school dress code[6]. It had been signed by almost our whole class, but it hadn't been given to the principal yet. We traced[7] all the names onto another sheet of paper, which said: "We, the undersigned, do hereby declare that Miriam Laker is weird, and do hereby announce that we hate her." Julie put that little gem[8] in Miriam's locker, just before biology class.

We waited in the biology room for Miriam to come in. We wanted to see how she had taken our last surprise. The tardy bell rang, but Miriam still hadn't come. "Maybe she isn't here today", Julie whispered to me. "She's never been late for a class before."

The period was almost over when we heard the rescue squad[9] arrive at school. Our teacher left the room to find out what had happened. I could hear him talking to another teacher in the hall.

"What's all this about?" our teacher asked.

"Oh, some girl – last name's Laker, I think – locked herself in the Home Ec[10] room. She turned on the gas from all four stoves. They got her out just in time." "Did you hear that?" I asked Julie. She nodded in amazement.[11] "Well," I whispered, "I always knew that anyone who wrote poetry would come to a bad end."

We began to laugh.

What unkind things do the girls do to Miriam during the next few days?

Find out why Miriam does not attend the biology class.

Would you have expected this reaction?

[1]**marble** small, coloured ball made of glass – [2]**principal** headmaster – [3]**voodoo** *Zauberei, Hexerei* – [4]**cute** (AE) pretty – [5]**petition** a request or demand – [6]**school dress code** rules that say what kind of clothing pupils are allowed to wear at school – [7]**to trace** to copy using a thin piece of paper placed over the original – [8]**gem** a thing of value – [9]**rescue squad** group especially trained in giving medical aid – [10]**Home EC** abbreviation for Home Economics, a course in home making skills – [11]**amazement** surprise

The nasty tricks – action and characters

Action, in fictional texts, is everything that happens in the story. It may be external, when the writer describes what the characters do, or it may be internal, when the writer shows the thoughts of the characters.
A **character** is a person who takes part in the action of a fictional text.

What nasty tricks do Karen and Julie play on Miriam? How does Miriam react? Draw a table like this and fill it in.

tricks	Miriam's reaction	Karen's and Julie's feelings
1		
2		
3		
4		

The three girls' behaviour

1. What do you think about Karen's and Julie's behaviour?
2. How would you have reacted in Miriam's place?

The theme of the story

The **theme** is the main generalized idea which the writer wants to present in his story. As the theme is usually not stated directly, the reader has to figure it out. One way of discovering the theme of a story is to consider what happens to the main character(s) and what it all means to him/her/them.

In your opinion, what is the basic theme of this short story?

Your ideas?

1. What do you think Miriam will tell her mother after her rescue?
2. Imagine the nasty tricks are discovered and the two girls are questioned by the principal. Prepare the roles of the principal, Julie and Karen and then act the scene.
3. Despite their reaction in the biology room Karen and Julie are now sorry for their behaviour and Karen wants to write a letter of apology to Miriam. Can you write the letter for her? (for help see pp. 76f.)

The Big Race Toby Sweet

Write before you read:

The following short story is about a swimming race. Before you read it, imagine that you are a reporter on a local newspaper that needs a ten-line article about a swimming race for the pupils of the town's schools. The following words and phrases may help you to write this article for the newspaper:

the swimming race
to compete
the club coach
two boys
the winner's block
fast
to concentrate
to encourage
a warming-up run
to present the winners with their medals
the father

Before you start writing, put the words and phrases above into a logical order (e.g. by numbering them). Don't forget to find a good headline for your article! (for help see pp. 78f.)

Before you read the text:
In the story you will meet three people. Pay attention to how they behave and what they say or think. You DON'T have to understand every detail.

The day of my swimming race was wet and dreary[1]. I was due to[2] swim two lengths' backstroke[3] at Chester-le-Street that afternoon.

As I walked into the changing rooms, taking a basket for my clothes on the way, I noticed a man and a boy sitting in

What information do you get in the first three lines?

[1]**dreary** dull and depressing – [2]**I was due to** I was expected to – [3]**backstroke** *Rückenschwimmen*

one corner, talking. I recognised the boy – he was called Gordon Hayes and I had swum against him before. He was fast – his best time for two lengths' backstroke was only one second slower than mine. He was tall with long legs and strong muscles. He had a pleasant[1] face which was topped by a shock[2] of dark brown hair. The man, who I assumed[3] was his father, was the opposite. He was short and stocky[4] with an almost square[5] face and a rapidly receding hairline[6]. I stood still, just out of their line of vision[7]. Something told me I should not disturb them. I heard the end of the conversation, although I had no real desire to spy on[8] them.

Gordon's father said, "If you divven't[9] win that race I'll really belt yer one[10]!"

"But, Dad ..."

"No buts. You can beat that lad from Durham."

"But I can't."

"You will or else."

Then his father stomped off[11], leaving Gordon curled up[12] in the corner, shaking like a leaf. I walked up to him and said innocently[13], "What's the matter?"

"It's him. He says he'll hit me if I don't beat you in the backstroke."

"I'm sure he wouldn't. You are his son."

"He will."

"Well, if you just do your best that's all anyone can ask for."

"My best won't be good enough", he said hopelessly.

What is your impression of the two boys and Gordon's father?

I finished getting changed into my team trunks[14] and, with my bag slung over my shoulder, walked past the cubicles[15], through the footbath and onto the poolside. The pool was 25 metres long and had six lanes. I walked over to the place where all the other swimmers from Durham had gathered[16] and let my bag fall heavily onto a bench. Then I strolled[17] over to Lane One and dived in. The water felt freezing – so cold I could hardly breathe. I swam up and down vacantly[18] for a few lengths, my mind always thinking about one thing – Gordon Hayes and his father's threats[19] if he did not win the race. I came out of my reverie[20] to hear a voice shouting my name. I looked up to see the club coach standing on the poolside calling to me to come and do a timed one length

[1]**pleasant** nice, friendly – [2]**a shock** a mop *(Haar)Wust* – [3]**to assume** to think – [4]**stocky** (of people) short and strong – [5]**square** the opposite of "round" – [6]**with a rapidly receding hairline** losing one's hair – [7]**just out of their line of vision** where they just couldn't see – [8]**to spy on sb.** to try to find out about so./sth. without being caught – [9]**divven't** (dialect) don't – [10]**I'll really belt yer one** (dialect/slang) I'll hit you really hard – [11]**to stomp off** to go away, walking heavily – [12]**to curl up** to sit with your knees under your chin – [13]**innocent** here: as if I hadn't heard anything – [14]**trunks** shorts for swimming – [15]**cubicle** here: changing room – [16]**to gather** to come together – [17]**to stroll** to walk slowly – [18]**vacantly** here: in a daydream – [19]**threat** a warning that sb. will hurt you if you do not do what he or she wants – [20]**reverie** daydream

21 stören

sprint to see if I was fully loosened out[1]. I swam to the end and crouched in the backstroke start position.

The coach barked[2], "Take your marks."

I tensed.[3]

"Go!"

I pushed off from the side with a flurry of water[4] kicked by my feet. My back dive had left me about one foot under the water so I kicked to the surface[5] and started using my arms as well as my legs. I swam as fast as I could for the other end and when my hand hit the end, the coach's finger hit the "stop" button on the stop-watch. He looked at my time.

"Hmmmm. 15.74 seconds. That's good. Go and put your tracksuit[6] on and keep warm. You don't swim till the fifth event[7]."

I walked over to my bag and took out my towel and tracksuit. I dried myself off, put on my tracksuit and sat down. I made myself as comfortable as I could – I sat on my towel to ease[8] the hardness of the bench and leant against my near empty bag to relax until my race. All the heats[9] preceding[10] mine passed one after the other as if only one race was being swum again and again. The coach approached[11] me and said, "It's nearly time for your race so you had better do some loosening exercises[12]."

I got up slowly and began to swing my arms to loosen them out. Then I bent over and touched my toes ten times to loosen my stomach muscles and the backs of my legs. I sat down again and went over the coming race in my mind, to plan my strategy. Then I remembered Gordon Hayes. I saw a picture in my mind of his father raising his fist. I tried to concentrate on the race but I found that I could not.

At last it was time for the race. I stood behind the starting block of Lane Three as a woman came to each swimmer in turn and took their entry cards so that their times could be recorded[13]. As she came up to me I held out my card ready. I looked along the line of swimmers but I did not know any of them except[14] Gordon Hayes who was in Lane 4, next to me.

The starter blew his whistle for silence and told us to jump into the water. I jumped in last and went down to the bottom, gave a big kick and was up to the surface again. I caught hold of the side just as the starter said, "Take your marks."

Again I tensed waiting for the gun. When it came the line of swimmers all did a back dive[15] away from the wall. I did not go as deep as I had in the warm-up so I did not have to

What are the boy's chances of winning the race?

Why is it so difficult for the boy to prepare for the race?

[1]**to be fully loosened out** to have warmed up completely – [2]**to bark** (e.g. dogs bark) – [3]**to tense** *sich anspannen* – [4]**a flurry of water** water turned into little waves and foam *(Schaum)* – [5]**surface** *Oberfläche* – [6]**tracksuit** sports clothes that keep you warm – [7]**event** here: race – [8]**to ease** here: to make feel sth. softer – [9]**heat** *Vorlauf* – [10]**to precede** to come before – [11]**to approach** to come up to – [12]**loosening exercices** warming-up exercises – [13]**to record** here: to write down – [14]**except** but not – [15]**back dive** the typical way of starting a backstroke race

kick as hard to reach the surface. It was only two lengths so I started swimming flat out straight from the start. I looked up and saw the flags which meant that I was near the end of the first length. My left hand found the wall. I spun my body round[1] on my back, flicked[2] my legs over and pushed off from the side. As I surfaced[3] I quickly glanced at the spectators' gallery. There I saw Mr Hayes shouting at Gordon to go faster. I looked to my left and saw Gordon only a half of a body behind. No one else was anywhere near us. Again I saw the flags and behind them Mr Hayes's shouting mouth and threatening[4] fist. I slowed down and saw Gordon catch up[5] and swim past me to finish a split second[6] ahead. I climbed out of the water, panting[7] heavily, and shook Gordon's hand.

The officials lost no time in presenting us with our medals. As I stood on the second place block and looked up to see Gordon on the winner's block I felt a sharp pang of regret[8] that I had let him win. However, when I looked up to the spectators' gallery and saw Mr Hayes smiling for once in his life I thought it was worth it.

?

I was wrong. As we were walking away from the podium Gordon turned to me with an unpleasant sneer on his face and said, „You're pathetic, I beat you by miles. I don't know how you ever beat me before. Well, you're never going to again. So there!"

What happens during the race?

Describe the boy's mixed feelings after the race.

How might this story end? Write five to ten sentences.

Did you expect this ending? Compare it with your own ideas.

[1]**to spin round** to turn round very quickly – [2]**to flick over** to turn over very quickly – [3]**to surface** to come to the surface *(Oberfläche)* – [4]**to threaten** to express a threat (cf. p. 11) – [5]**to catch up** to come closer – [6]**a split second** less than a second – [7]**to pant** to breathe heavily – [8]**regret** feeling sorry

The characters in a story

Characterization means the presentation of a character's outward appearance[1], behaviour[2], thoughts and/or feelings.
The author may present the characters in two ways:
– directly by describing them, or explicit
– indirectly through their actions and words. implicit

1. How are the two boys and Gordon's father characterized? What impression do they make on you? (for help see pp. 71 ff.)
2. Do you think that the boy's bitter experience will change his character?

How to tell a story: The plot

The way the action in a short story is structured and centred around the conflict so that suspense[3] is created is called **plot**. A plot has several stages: exposition (introduction to the main characters, the setting, etc.), rising action (developing conflict), climax (the moment when the conflict is most intense), turning point (the point at which an important change takes place), falling action (reduction in suspense) and dénouement[4] (solution to the problem).

This structure can be shown like this:

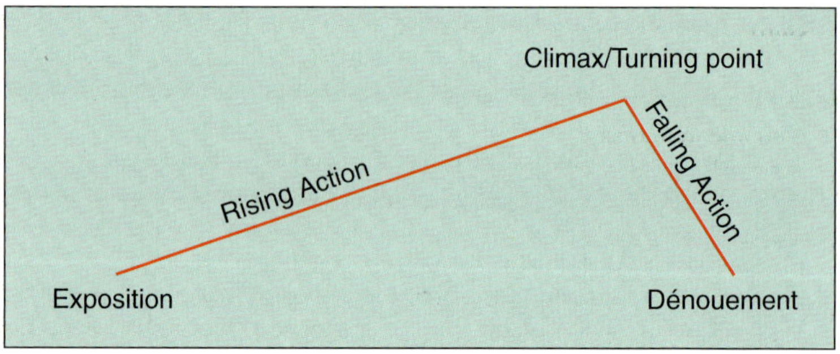

Use this pattern to work out the structure of *The Big Race* and give each part a heading.

Fiction or real life?

1. The author of this story was a boy of twelve at the time. Speculate on whether this text is purely fictional or not and give reasons for your ideas.
2. Can you describe the differences between the newspaper article that you wrote before reading the story and the story itself?

[1]**outward appearance** what people look like – [2]**behaviour** how people act – [3]**suspense** *Spannung* – [4]**dénouement** [dei'nu:'mãŋ] the ending of a fictional text

Manhood John Wain

Before you read the story:

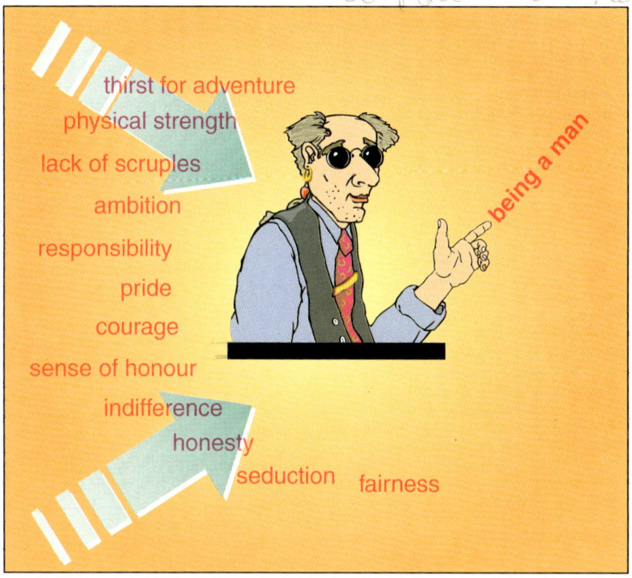

Which of these characteristic features do you think are typical of a man? Can you imagine situations where he shows them?

When you read the story find out which of these features apply to the father.

Swiftly free-wheeling[1], their breath coming easily, the man and the boy steered their bicycles down the short dip[2] which led them from woodland into open country. Then they looked ahead and saw that the road began to climb.

"Now, Rob,", said Mr Willison, settling his plump[3] haunches[4] firmly on the saddle, "just up that rise and we'll get off and have a good rest."

"Can't we rest now?" the boy asked. "My legs feel all funny. As if they're turning to water."

"Rest at the top," said Mr Willison firmly. "Remember what I told you? The first thing any athlete[5] has to learn is to break the fatigue[6] barrier."

"I've broken it already. I was feeling tired when we were going along the main road and I –"

"When fatigue sets in, the thing to do is to keep going until it wears off[7]. Then you get your second wind and your second endurance[8]."

"I've already done that."

*

Why doesn't Mr Willison allow his son to rest?

What do you think will happen next?

[1]**to free-wheel** to ride a bicycle without pedalling – [2]**dip** downward slope – [3]**plump** pleasantly fat – [4]**haunch** part of the body round the hips – [5]**athlete** ['æθli:t] – [6]**fatigue** extreme tiredness – [7]**to wear off** to pass away, to stop – [8]**endurance** Ausdauer

"Up we go,", said Mr Willison, "and at the top we'll have a good rest." He panted[1] slightly and stood on his pedals, causing his machine to sway[2] from side to side in a laboured[3] manner. Rob, falling silent, pushed doggedly[4] at his pedals. Slowly, the pair wavered[5] up the straight road to the top. Once there, Mr Willison dismounted with exaggerated[6] steadiness, laid his bicycle carefully on its side, and spread his jacket on the ground before sinking down to rest. Rob slid hastily from the saddle and flung himself full-length on the grass.

"Don't lie there,", said his father. "You'll catch cold."

"I'm all right. I'm warm."

"Come and sit on this. When you're over-heated, that's just when you're prone to[7] –."

"I'm all right. Dad. I want to lie here, my back aches."

"Your back needs strengthening, that's why it aches. It's a pity we don't live near a river where you could get some rowing."

The boy did not answer, and Mr Willison, aware that he was beginning to sound like a nagging[8], over-anxious parent, allowed himself to be defeated and did not press the suggestion about Rob's coming to sit on his jacket. Instead, he waited a moment and then glanced at his watch.

"Twenty to twelve. We must get going in a minute."

"*What?* I thought we were going to have a rest."

"Well, we're having one, aren't we?" said Mr Willison reasonably.

"I've got my breath back, so surely you must have."

"My back still aches. I want to lie here a bit."

"Sorry," said Mr Willison, getting up and moving over to his bicycle. "We've got at least twelve miles to do and lunch is at one."

"Dad, why did we have to come so far if we've got to get back for one o'clock? I know, let's find a telephone box and ring up Mum and tell her we –."

"Nothing doing[9]. There's no reason why two fit men shouldn't cycle twelve miles in an hour and ten minutes."

"But we've already done about a million miles."

"We've done about fourteen, by my estimation[10]," said Mr Willison stiffly. "What's the good of going for a bike ride if you don't cover a bit of distance?"

He picked up his bicycle and stood waiting. Rob, with his hand over his eyes, lay motionless on the grass. His legs looked thin and white among the rich grass.

"Come on, Rob."

What is Mr Willison's attitude towards cycling? How does Rob feel? (ll. 23–59)

[1]**to pant** to take short, quick breaths, especially after some physical effort – [2]**to sway** to move slowly from one side to another – [3]**laboured** showing signs of difficulty – [4]**dogged** ['dɔgid] *verbissen, hartnäckig* – [5]**to waver** to move unsteadily – [6]**exaggerated** *übertrieben* – [7]**to be prone to** to be likely to – [8]**to nag** to criticize continuously, often without reason – [9]**nothing doing** (col.) *geht nicht* – [10]**estimation** calculation

The boy showed no sign of having heard. Mr Willison got on to his bicycle and began to ride slowly away. "Rob," he called over his shoulder. "I'm going."

Rob lay like a sullen[1] corpse[2] by the roadside. He looked horribly like the victim[3] of an accident, unmarked but dead from internal[4] injuries. Mr Willison cycled fifty yards, then a hundred, then turned in a short, irritable[5] circle and came back to where his son lay.

"Rob, is there something the matter or are you just being awkward?"[6]

The boy removed his hand and looked up into his father's face. His eyes were surprisingly mild: there was no fire of rebellion in them.

"I'm tired and my back aches. I can't go on yet."

Rob is worn out. How does Mr Willison persuade him to get on his bike again?

"Look, Rob", said Mr Willison gently, "I wasn't going to tell you this, because I meant it to be a surprise, but when you get home you'll find a present waiting for you."

"What kind of present?"

"Something very special I've bought for you. The man's coming this morning to fix it up. That's one reason why I suggested a bike ride this morning. He'll have done it by now."

"What is it?"

"Aha! It's a surprise. Come on, get on your bike and let's go home and see." Rob sat up, then slowly clambered[7] to his feet. "Isn't there a short cut[8] home?"

"I'm afraid not. It's only twelve miles."

Rob said nothing.

"And a lot of that's downhill," Mr Willison added brightly. His own legs were tired and his muscles fluttered unpleasantly. In addition, he suddenly realized he was very thirsty. Rob, still without speaking, picked up his bicycle, and they pedalled away.

"Where is he?" Mrs Willison asked, coming into the garage.

"Gone up to his room," said Mr Willison. He doubled his fist and gave the punch-ball a thudding[9] blow. "Seems to have fixed it pretty firmly. You gave him the instructions, I suppose."

"What's he doing up in his room? It's lunch-time."

"He said he wanted to rest a bit."

"I hope you're satisfied," said Mrs Willison. "A lad of thirteen, nearly fourteen years of age, just when he should have a really big appetite, and when the lunch is put on the table he's *resting* –"

"Now look, I know what I'm –"

[1]**sullen** silent and angry – [2]**corpse** dead body – [3]**victim** *Opfer* – [4]**internal** inside the body – [5]**irritable** here: showing that he is angry – [6]**just being awkward** just not cooperating – [7]**to clamber** to climb with difficulty – [8]**short cut** quicker, more direct way – [9]**to thud** to make a dull sound

"Lying down in his room, resting, too tired to eat because you've dragged him up hill and down dale[1] on one of your –."

"We did nothing that couldn't be reasonably expected of a boy of his age."

"How do you know?" Mrs Willison demanded. "You never did anything of that kind when you were a boy. How do you know what can be reasonably –?"

"Now look," said Mr Willison again. "When I was a boy, it was study, study, study all the time, with the fear of unemployment and insecurity[2] in everybody's mind. I was never even given a bicycle. I never boxed, I never rowed, I never did anything to develop my physique[3]. It was just work, work, work, pass this exam, get that certificate. Well, I did it and now I'm qualified[4] and in a secure job. But you know as well as I do that they let me down. Nobody encouraged me to build myself up."

"Well, what does it matter? You're all right –."

"Grace!" Mr Willison interrupted sharply. "I am not all right and you know it. I am under average[5] height, my chest is flat and I'm –."

"What nonsense. You're taller than I am and I'm –."

"No son of mine is going to grow up with the same wretched[6] physical heritage[7] that I –."

"No, he'll just have heart disease through overtaxing[8] his strength, because you haven't got the common sense to –."

"His heart is one hundred per cent all right. Not three weeks have gone by since the doctor looked at him."

"Well, why does he get so over-tired if he's all right? Why is he lying down now instead of coming to the table, a boy of his age?"

A slender shadow blocked part of the dazzling sun in the doorway. Looking up simultaneously[9], the Willisons greeted their son.

"Lunch ready, Mum? I'm hungry."

"Ready when you are," Grace Willison beamed[10]. "Just wash your hands and come to the table."

"Look, Rob," said Mr Willison. "If you hit it with your left hand and then catch it on the rebound[11] with your right, it's excellent ring training." He dealt the punch-ball two amateurish blows. "That's what they call a right cross," he said.

"I think it's fine. I'll have some fun with it," said Rob. He watched mildly as his father peeled off the padded mittens[12].

Why is Mr Willison so keen on his son being good at sports?

[1]**up hill and down dale** up hills and down into valleys – [2]**insecurity** *Unsicherheit* – [3]**physique** the shape and appearance of a human body – [4]**to be qualified** to have the necessary qualifications – [5]**average** normal – [6]**wretched** miserable – [7]**heritage** *Erbschaft* – [8]**to overtax** to do more than one is really able to do – [9]**simultaneously** at the same time – [10]**to beam** to smile happily – [11]**on the rebound** when moving back – [12]**mitten** here: boxing glove

"Here, slip these on," said Mr Willison. "They're just training gloves. They harden your fists. Of course, we can get a pair of proper gloves later. But these are specially for use with the ball."

"Lunch," called Mrs Willison from the house.

"Take a punch at it," Mr Willison urged.

"Let's go and eat."

"Go on. One punch before you go in. I haven't seen you hit it yet."

Rob took the gloves, put on the right-hand one, and gave the punch-ball one conscientious[1] blow, aiming at the exact centre.

"Now let's go in," he said.

"Lunch!"

"All right. We're coming ..."

Why has Mr Willison bought a punch-ball for Rob?

*

"Five feet eight, Rob," said Mr Willison, folding up the wooden ruler.

"You're taller than I am. This is a great landmark."[2]

"Only *just* taller."

"But you're growing all the time. Now all you have to do is to start growing outwards as well as upwards. We'll have you in the middle of that scrum[3]. The heaviest forward in the pack."

Rob picked up his shirt and began uncertainly poking his arms into the sleeves.

"When do they pick the team?" Mr Willison asked. "I should have thought they'd have done it by now."

"They have done it," said Rob. He bent down to pick up his socks from under a chair.

"They have? And you –?"

"I wasn't selected," said the boy, looking intently at the socks as if trying to detect minute[4] differences in colour and weave.

Mr Willison opened his mouth, closed it again, and stood for a moment looking out of the window. Then he gently laid his hand on his son's shoulder. "Bad luck," he said quietly.

"I tried hard," said Rob quickly.

"I'm sure you did."

"I played my hardest in the trial games."

"It's just bad luck," said Mr Willison. "It could happen to anybody."

There was silence as they both continued with their dressing. A faint smell of frying rose into the air, and they could hear Mrs Willison laying the table for breakfast.

Why is Mr Willison a little disappointed?

How does Rob try to cheer him up?

[1]**conscientious** here: well-aimed – [2]**landmark** event that marks a turning-point – [3]**scrum** a pack or a group of rugby players who try to push the other team's scrum off the ball – [4]**minute** [mai'nju:t] very small

"That's it, then, for this season," said Mr Willison, as if to himself.

"I forgot to tell you, though," said Rob, "I was selected for the boxing team."

"You *were*? I didn't know the school had one."

"It's new. Just formed. They had some trials for it at the end of last term. I found my punching was better than most people's because I'd been getting plenty of practice with the ball."

Mr Willison put out a hand and felt Rob's biceps[1]. "Not bad, not bad at all," he said critically. "But if you're going to be a boxer and represent the school, you'll need more power up there. I tell you what. We'll train together."

"That'll be fun," said Rob. "I'm training at school too."

"What weight do they put you in?"

"It isn't weight, it's age. Under fifteen. Then when you get over fifteen you get classified into weights."

"Well," said Mr Willison, tying his tie, "you'll be in a good position for the under-fifteens. You've got six months to play with. And there's no reason why you shouldn't steadily put muscle on all the time. I suppose you'll be entered as a team, for tournaments and things?"

"Yes. There's a big one at the end of next term. I'll be in that."

Confident, joking, they went down to breakfast. "Two eggs for Rob, Mum," said Mr Willison. "He's in training. He's going to be a heavyweight."

"A heavyweight what?" Mrs Willison asked, teapot in hand.

"Boxer," Rob smiled.

Grace Willison put down the teapot, her lips compressed[2], and looked from one to the other. "*Boxing?*" she repeated.

"Boxing," Mr Willison replied calmly.

"Over my dead body," said Mrs Willison. "That's one sport I'm definite that he's never going in for."

"Too late. They've picked him for the under-fifteens. He's had trials and everything."

"Is this true, Rob?" she demanded.

"Yes," said the boy, eating rapidly.

"Well, you can just tell them you're dropping it. Baroness Summerskill[3] –."

"To hell with Baroness Summerskill!" her husband shouted. "The first time he gets a chance to do something, the first time he gets picked for a team and given a chance to show what he's made of, and you have to bring up Baroness Summerskill."

[1]**biceps** ['baiseps] – [2]**to compress** to press together – [3]**Baroness Summerskill** former Labour M. P. who was an opponent of boxing

"But it injures their brains! All those blows on the front of the skull[1]. I've read about it –."

"Injures their brains!" Mr Willison snorted[2]. "Has it injured Ingemar Johansson's brain? Why, he's one of the acutest[3] business men in the world!"

"Rob," said Mrs Willison steadily, "when you get to school, go and see the sports master and tell him you're giving up boxing."

"There isn't a sports master. All the masters do bits of it at different times."

"There must be one who's in charge of the boxing. All you have to do is tell him –."

"Are you ready, Rob?" said Mr Willison. "You'll be late for school if you don't go."

"I'm in plenty of time, Dad. I haven't finished my breakfast."

"Never mind, push along, old son. You've had your egg and bacon, that's what matters. I want to talk to your mother."

Cramming[4] a piece of dry toast into his mouth, the boy picked up his satchel and wandered from the room. Husband and wife sat back, glaring[5] hot-eyed at each other.

The quarrel began, and continued for many days. In the end it was decided that Rob should continue boxing until he had represented the school at the tournament in March of the following year, and should then give it up.

*

"Ninety-six, ninety-seven, ninety-eight, ninety-nine, a hundred," Mr Willison counted. "Right, that's it. Now go and take your shower and get into bed."

"I don't feel tired, honestly," Rob protested.

"Who's manager here, you or me?" Mr Willison asked bluffly[6]. "I'm in charge of training and you can't say my methods don't work. Fifteen solid weeks and you start questioning my decisions on the very night of the fight?"

"It just seems silly to go to bed when I'm not –."

"My dear Rob, please trust me. No boxer ever went into a big fight without spending an hour or two in bed, resting, just before going to his dressing-room."

"All right. But I bet none of the others are bothering to do all this."

"That's exactly why you're going to be better than the others. Now go and get your shower before you catch cold. Leave the skipping-rope[7], I'll put it away."

After Rob had gone, Mr Willison folded the skipping-rope

✓ How does Mr Willison feel about his son's boxing career?

[1]**skull** *Schädel* – [2]**to snort** to force air out through the nose – [3]**acute** clever – [4]**to cram** tu push too much into something – [5]**to glare** to look angrily at somebody for a long time – [6]**bluff** behaving in a loud, cheerful way, without always considering the way other people feel – [7]**skipping-rope** *Springseil*

into a neat[1] ball and packed it away in the case that contained the boy's gloves, silk dressing gown, lace-up[2] boxing boots, and trunks with the school badge[3] sewn into the correct position on the right leg. There would be no harm in a little skipping, to limber up[4] and conquer his nervousness while waiting to go on. Humming, he snapped down the catches[5] of the small leather case and went into the house.

Mrs Willison did not lift her eyes from the television set as he entered. "All ready now, Mother," said Mr Willison. "He's going to rest in bed now, and go along at about six o'clock. I'll go with him and wait till the doors open to be sure of a ringside seat." He sat down on the sofa beside his wife, and tried to put his arm round her. "Come on, love," he said coaxingly[6]. "Don't spoil my big night."

She turned to him and he was startled[7] to see her eyes brimming[8] with angry tears. "What about my big night?" she asked, her voice harsh. "Fourteen years ago, remember? When he came into the world."

"Well, what about it?" Mr Willison parried[9], uneasily aware that the television set was quacking and signalling on the fringe[10] of his attention, turning the scene from clumsy[11] tragedy into a clumsier farce.

"Why didn't you tell me then?" she sobbed. "Why did you let me have a son if all you were interested in was having him punched to death by a lot of rough bullet-headed louts[12] who –."

"Take a grip on yourself, Grace. A punch on the nose won't hurt him."

"You're an unnatural father," she keened[13]. "I don't know how you can bear to send him into that ring to be beaten and thumped[14] – Oh, why can't you stop him now? Keep him at home? There's no *law* that compels us to –."

"That's where you're wrong, Grace," said Mr Willison sternly. "There is a law. The unalterable[15] law of nature that says that the young males of the species[16] indulge[17] in manly trials of strength. Think of all the other lads who are going into the ring tonight. D'you think their mothers are sitting about crying and kicking up a fuss[18]? No – they're proud to have strong, masculine sons who can stand up in the ring and take a few punches."

"Go away, please," said Mrs Willison, sinking back with closed eyes. "Just go right away and don't come near me until it's all over."

"Grace!"

[1]**neat** tidy – [2]**to lace** to fasten with laces – [3]**badge** *Abzeichen* – [4]**to limber up** *Lockerungsübungen machen* – [5]**catch** a small lock or sth. similar for fastening sth. – [6]**coaxing** trying to persuade so. who is unwilling to do sth. – [7]**startled** surprised or shocked – [8]**to brim** to be very full of sth. – [9]**to parry** here: to answer – [10]**fringe** edge – [11]**clumsy** here: not as written by a good dramatist – [12]**lout** a rude man or boy – [13]**to keen** to lament – [14]**to thump** to strike heavily – [15]**unalterable** what cannot be changed – [16]**species** *Art* – [17]**to indulge in** here: to take part in – [18]**to kick up a fuss** *sich anstellen*

"Please. Please leave me alone. I can't bear to look at you and I can't bear to hear you."

"You're hysterical," said Mr Willison bitterly. Rising, he went out into the hall and called up the stairs. "Are you in bed, Rob?"

There was a slight pause and Rob's voice called faintly, "Could you come up, Dad?"

"Come up? Why? Is something the matter?"

"Could you come up?"

Mr Willison ran up the stairs. "What is it?" he panted. "D'you want something?"

"I think I've got appendicitis[1]," said Rob. He lay squinting[2] among the pillows, his face suddenly narrow and crafty[3].

How does Rob behave on the night of the boxing tournament? How does his father react?

"I don't believe you", said Mr Willison shortly. "I've supervised your training for fifteen weeks and I know you're as fit as a fiddle[4]. You can't possibly have anything wrong with you."

"I've got a terrible pain in my side," said Rob. "Low down on the right-hand side. That's where appendicitis comes, isn't it?"

Mr Willison sat down on the bed. "Listen, Rob," he said. "Don't do this to me. All I'm asking you to do is to go into the ring and have one bout[5].

You've been picked for the school team and everyone's depending on you."

"I'll die if you don't get the doctor."Rob suddenly hissed. "Mum!" he shouted.

Mrs Willison came bounding[6] up the stairs. "What is it, my pet?"

"My stomach hurts. Low down on the right-hand side."

"Appendicitis!" She whirled to face Mr Willison. "That's what comes of your foolishness!"

"I don't believe it", said Mr Willison. He went out of the bedroom and down the stairs. The television was still jabbering[7] in the living-room, and for fifteen minutes Mr Willison forced himself to sit staring at the strident[8] puppets, glistening in metallic light, as they enacted their Lilliputian rituals. Then he went up to the bedroom again. Mrs Willison was bathing Rob's forehead.

"His temperature's normal," she said.

"Of course his temperature's normal," said Mr Willison. "He doesn't want to fight, that's all."

"Fetch the doctor," said a voice from under the cold flannel that swathed[9] Rob's face.

[1]**appendicitis** [ə'pendi'saitis] *Blinddarmentzündung* – [2]**to squint** to look with half-shut eyes – [3]**crafty** clever but not honest – [4]**to be fit as a fiddle** to be in excellent condition – [5]**bout** boxing match – [6]**to bound** to jump – [7]**to jabber** to talk quickly and excitedly – often with other people not listening – [8]**strident** speaking in too loud voices – [9]**to swathe** to cover

"We will, pet, if you don't get better very soon," said Mrs Willison, darting[1] a murderous glance at her husband.

Mr Willison slowly went downstairs. For a moment he stood looking at the telephone, then picked it up and dialled the number of the grammar school. No one answered. He replaced the receiver, went to the foot of the stairs and called, "What's the name of the master in charge of[2] this tournament?"

"I don't know," Rob called weakly.

"You told me you'd been training with Mr Granger," Mr Willison called. "Would he know anything about it?"

Rob did not answer, so Mr Willison looked up all the Grangers in the telephone book. There were four in the town, but only one was M. A. "That's him," said Mr Willison. With lead in his heart and ice in his fingers, he dialled the number.

Mrs Granger fetched Mr Granger. Yes, he taught at the school. He was the right man. What could he do for Mr Willison?

"It's about tonight's boxing tournament."

"Sorry, what? The line's bad."

"*Tonight's boxing tournament.*"

"Have you got the right person?"

"You teach my son, Rob – we've just agreed on that. Well, it's about the boxing tournament he's supposed to be taking part in tonight."

"Where?"

"Where? At the school, of course. He's representing the under-fifteens."

There was a pause. "I'm not quite sure what mistake you're making Mr Willison, but I think you've got hold of the wrong end of at least one stick[3]." A hearty, defensive laugh. "If Rob belongs to a boxing club it's certainly news to me, but in any case it can't be anything to do with the school. We don't go in for boxing."

"Don't go in for it?"

"We don't offer it. It's not in our curriculum[4]."

"Oh," said Mr Willison. "Oh. Thank you, I must have – well, thank you."

"Not at all. I'm glad to answer any queries[5]. Everything's all right, I trust?"

"Oh, yes," said Mr Willison, "yes, thanks. Everything's all right."

He put down the telephone, hesitated, then turned and began slowly to climb the stairs.

A What might Mr Willison think and feel when he puts down the telephone receiver?

[1]**to dart** to send suddenly and quickly – [2]**to be in charge of** to be in a position of control or command – [3]**to get hold of the wrong end of the stick** to misunderstand sth. – [4]**curriculum** subjects taught at a particular school, college, etc. – [5]**query** question

Your first reaction to the story

What are your impressions of Rob, his father and his mother? Use a mind map to organize your ideas.

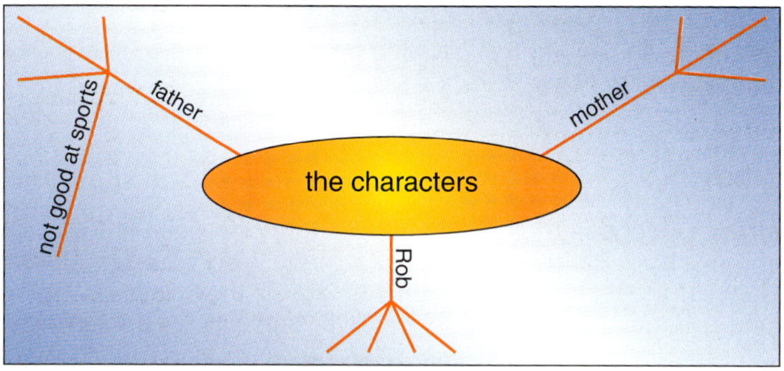

The relationship between Mr Willison and his son

Mr Willison's various reasons and plans for his attempts to turn Rob into an athlete	His methods	Rob's reactions to his father's attempts

Put your ideas in a table like this.

Your opinion of Mr Willison

1. Has the definition of manhood that you formed before reading the story changed?
2. What kind of man is Mr Willison? Try to characterize him. (For help see pp. 71 ff.)
3. What do you think of his way of bringing up his son?

How to tell a story: Point of view

The **point of view** is the perspective from which a story is presented. The story can be told by a first-person narrator[1] ("I" as in the story *Locker 160*) or by a third-person narrator ("he" or "she" as in the story *Manhood*). The narrator can be a character in or outside the story.

Compare the way in which the stories *Locker 160* and *Manhood* are told and try to explain the effect of the different modes of narration on the reader.

Writing options

1. Rob regularly keeps a diary. Can you choose one day during the period which the story covers and write a diary entry for him? (For help see pp. 77 f.)
2. The story has an open ending. How might the relationship between Mr Willison and his son develop?

[1]**narrator** sb. who tells a story

Project Write your own story.

Try to tell a story along the following guidelines (for help see p. 75). You can work on your own or in pairs.

Characters

Margaret Evans is a girl of about fourteen. She goes to the local comprehensive school. Sarah Jane is her best friend. Very often Margaret and Sarah Jane wear the same clothes. Some time ago, they also had the same short haircut. Margaret's aunt gave her a silver bracelet[1] for her birthday.

Sarah Jane is in the same class as Margaret. She now has long plaits[2]. She likes Margaret very much. The two friends spend a lot of time together. Two years ago Sarah Jane's grandmother gave her a bracelet for Christmas that looks a lot like Margaret's.

Situation

At school, one day, Margaret discovers that her bracelet is missing. She suspects[3] Sarah Jane of stealing it. Sarah Jane denies the charges[4]. An old school photo is important for the story's ending.

Some further suggestions

1. **Setting/circumstances:** a) In which room(s) of the school could the action take place? b) What could this/these room(s) look like? c) Think of the season, the weather, the time of the day, etc. d) How much time might be covered by the story? e) What could the two girls look like? f) What could the bracelet look like?
2. **Plot:** a) How, when and where does the story begin? b) How does it develop to a climax/turning point? c) What is its dénouement? (cf. information on p. 14)
3. **Characters/motivations:** a) How might Margaret feel when she discovers the loss of her bracelet? b) How could she react? c) Why may she suspect Sarah Jane of stealing it? d) How may Sarah Jane feel when her best friend accuses her of stealing her bracelet? e) How may she react? f) How could the relationship between the two girls develop during the story?
4. **Dialogue/thoughts:** a) What might the characters talk about? b) What might go on in their minds?
5. Find a **title** for your story.

[1]**bracelet** band or ring round the arm – [2]**plait** *Haarzopf* – [3]**to suspect sb. of** to think that sb. has done sth. wrong – [4]**to deny the charges** to say that you have not done what you are accused of

Unit 2 Love is ...

Getting into the Unit

This picture shows you the place where the play *Jumping* is set and the two characters you will meet.

Look at it carefully:
Does it make you curious about what will happen?
What questions would you like the play to answer?

Short Play

A **play** is a piece of literature that is written to be presented on a stage. Actors and actresses play the roles of the characters. A full-length play is divided into acts and scenes. A **short play** like "Jumping" is a one-act play that is not – except for radio plays – divided into smaller parts. In every play you will find the same elements as in a short story: theme, setting, characters and plot.

Jumping William Borden

The action takes place on a Minnesota Bridge during winter at the present time.

Characters:
JERRY – a man from San Francisco
DENISE – a woman from Minnesota

At rise: JERRY, wearing suit coat[1] or sport coat, enters quickly, determinedly[2], and heads straight for bridge railing. Steps up, gets ready to jump, holds his breath, closes his eyes – comic effect – stops, thinks, steps down, takes off shoes. Climbs up again, gets ready to jump, etc., stops. Unbuttons[3] coat, gets ready to jump, stops. Buttons coat, gets ready to jump, stops. Thinks. Steps down.

JERRY: I can never remember – do you take your coat off when you jump, or leave it on? If you leave it on, you sink faster. That would seem to be the point. But in the movies I think they take their coats off ... *(Ponders[4]. Blows on hands to warm them. Hits his head.)* Of course! You leave the coat, because you leave some identification[5] in the coat pocket! *(Looks through coat pockets.)* Otherwise, no one might even know ... and if no one knows – what's the point? *(Searching pants[6] pockets.)* I forgot my wallet[7]. A note! I've got to be sure she knows ... *(DENISE[8], bundled[9] in winter coat, mufflers[10], hat, enters, preoccupied[11], looking forlorn[12].)* Excuse me. *(DENISE, lost in her own thoughts, doesn't hear him.)* Excuse me? *(DENISE walks past him, not noticing him. JERRY touches her shoulder. She jumps.)*

DENISE: Oh! You scared[13] me.

JERRY: I just wondered if you had a piece of paper and a pen or pencil ... *(DENISE looks at him curiously.)* I want to write a note. Probably just my name ... address ... Social Se-

Stage directions are notes in a play that tell the actors how to speak and act. They also say what the characters and the stage should look like and where and when the action takes place.
Stage directions also help the reader, who cannot see the play performed on stage, to get a vivid idea of what is going on.

What information do these stage directions give you about the situation at the beginning of the play?

What is Jerry preparing to do? What is his problem?

How is Denise presented through the stage directions?

[1]**suit coat** a suit jacket – [2]**determined** here: not easy to stop – [3]**to unbutton** to open a coat or a jacket – [4]**to ponder** to think about sth. carefully – [5]**identification** [ai,dentifi'keiʃn] – [6]**pants** trousers – [7]**wallet** *Brieftasche* – [8]**Denise** [də'ni:z] – [9]**to be bundled in** to be wrapped up in – [10]**muffler** scarf – [11]**preoccupied** lost in one's thoughts – [12]**forlorn** lonely and unhappy – [13]**to scare** to frighten

curity[1] number ... bank account[2] number ... driver's license number ... telephone number ...

DENISE: Are you cashing a check[3]?

JERRY: No, I'm ... *DENISE looks through her purse[4]. Looks some more. JERRY waits ... waits ... looks over her shoulder ...)*

DENISE: Could you hold these? I'm sure I have a pen ... *(DENISE loads JERRY up with stuff from her purse. Finds a pen.) Here's a pen!* (DENISE *hands it to JERRY, but his hands are full. DENISE sticks the pen in JERRY'S mouth.)* I think I have a notepad[5] ... *(DENISE pulls more stuff from her purse, loads up JERRY, dumps out[6] her purse.)* I was sure I had a notepad ... *(JERRY sees a letter amidst the stuff dumped from her purse, drops the stuff in his hands, and picks up the letter.)*

JERRY: What about this?

Imagine this moment on stage. What is its effect?

DENISE: No! *(Grabs letter.)* Where's your coat? You'll catch pneumonia[7]! Frostbite[8]! *(JERRY laughs).*

JERRY: *(Grabs letter, tears off a corner, absentmindedly[9] stuffs letter in his pocket, writes on the corner.)* Frostbite? Pneumonia? Those maladies[10] don't scare me anymore, my dear. No more worries about carcinogens[11] for me. Cigarettes, power lines, nuclear reactors – I don't care.

DENISE: You don't care?

JERRY: I'm past caring[12]. *(Hands her pen.)* Here. Thanks a lot. Saved my life. *(Pause)* So to speak. *(JERRY puts corner in coat pocket. Looks around for a place to put the coat.)*

DENISE: You're past caring?

JERRY: Yes.

DENISE: That's despicable[13].

JERRY: What?

DENISE: No public spirit! No political consciousness[14]! No democratic responsibility[15].

JERRY: It's not that –

DENISE: You should be ashamed!

Why does Denise become so upset?

JERRY: No, you don't understand – you see, actually. I'm – I'm a –

DENISE: *(Putting things back into her purse.)* Haven't you ever stood up for what you believed in? Haven't you ever considered dying for a cause? You probably don't even vote! Are you registered to vote[16]?

JERRY: Well, no, I just –

DENISE: Would you like to join the Sierra Club? I have an ap-

[1]**social security** *Sozialversicherung* – [2]**bank account** *Bankkonto* – [3]**to cash a check (AE)** to get money for a cheque (BE) – [4]**purse (AE)** handbag – [5]**notepad** a small book in which you write things which you want to remember – [6]**to dump out** here: to empty – [7]**pneumonia** [nju'məʊniə] a dangerous illness of the lungs – [8]**frostbite** *Frostbeulen, Erfrierungen* – [9]**absentminded** not paying attention – [10]**malady** illness – [11]**carcinogens** *Krebs erregende Substanzen* – [12]**I'm past caring** I don't care any more – [13]**despicable** *verachtenswert* – [14]**consciousness** *Bewusstsein* – [15]**responsibility** *Verantwortung* – [16]**to be registered to vote** if you want to vote in the USA you must put your name on a list before election day

plication[1] in here. *(Looks through purse.)* Would you hold this? *(Looks through purse.)* Could you just hold these again? *(Loads him with stuff again. JERRY impatient – resigned[2] – impatient – edges toward[3] railing.)*

JERRY: Maybe you could mail[4] it to me.

DENISE: You won't regret it. (DENISE *beams at[5] him. He smiles back, waiting for her stuff, which she seems to have forgotten about.)* Well?

JERRY: Well?

DENISE: Give me your name and address, so I can mail you the application form.

JERRY: Oh! Sure. Do you have a piece of paper? Pen? *(DENISE looks in empty purse. They look at each other. Laugh. JERRY holds out stuff.)*

DENISE: Oh! *(Puts stuff back in her purse.)* I'm not myself tonight. I'm a little upset, in fact. I get politically involved[6] when I'm upset ... about personal matters ... When I was younger, I became a socialist ... after my fiancé[7] left me at the church. It takes my mind off my own troubles. If we had more personal problems, people would get more interested in politics, that's what I think. We could have a real democracy[8] if everybody's personal life was a mess[9]. Do you agree?

JERRY: Could you hold this? *(His coat.)*

DENISE: Not until I get your name and address and your solemn[10] promise to join.

JERRY: The Socialists?

DENISE: Sierra Club. I'm not *that* upset. I've had these rejections[11] before.

JERRY: Um – listen, could you just join for me?

DENISE: Oh, I couldn't do that. That's not democracy.

JERRY: I'm really cold.

DENISE: Well you silly goose! It's Minnesota! Where do you think your are, Florida?

JERRY: Actually, I just moved from San Francisco a few months ago. This is my first winter. And my last.

DENISE: Don't you like it here?

JERRY: It's not that. It's ... personal problems.

DENISE: *(Pause)* I could arrange for you to get in contact with the Socialist Workers Party. If it's a serious personal problem. If it's not too serious, probably volunteering[12] for the Republicans would do the trick[13].

JERRY: It's too serious for the Socialist Workers Party.

A moment of **comic relief** in a serious play amuses the audience. For a short time there is not so much tension. On the other hand comic relief also creates suspense because the development of the action is held up for a moment.

What makes this moment so funny?

Why are politics so important for Denise?

As you read the following passage (up to p. 31, l. 154) you will see that Jerry and Denise do not really understand each other. Take notes on what each character talks about.

[1]**application** (e.g. you write letters of application when you want to get a job) – [2]**resigned** [ri'zaind] – [3]**to edge toward** to move slowly towards – [4]**to mail** (for letters, etc.) to send by post – [5]**to beam at** to smile warmly at – [6]**to get involved** to take part in something because you believe in it – [7]**fiancé** [fi'ãn'sei] *Verlobter* – [8]**democracy** [di'mɔkrəsi] – [9]**to be a mess** to be disorganised, full of trouble and problems – [10]**solemn** here: formal, sincere – [11]**rejection** turning down, not accepting – [12]**volunteering** (offering) to do useful work without being paid – [13]**to do the trick** (colloquial) here: to help

The Sierra Club is an environmental organization.

DENISE: *(Long look. Looks around. Whisper.)* I cannot take you there myself, but I know a man who knows a man who can put you in touch with[1] the underground group ...

JERRY: No, no ...

DENISE: Left wing or right wing, whichever you prefer, it works the same, your personal problems melt away, you give yourself to a higher cause ...

JERRY: Just sign me up with the Sierra Club ... What did you say your name was?

DENISE: Denise.

JERRY: My name's Jerry. With a J.

DENISE: *(They shake hands.)* Your hand's so cold!

JERRY: Yes, I've been trying to – Would you hold this? *(His coat. She takes it.)*

DENISE: Put your coat on, for heaven's sake. Jerry! *(Jerry edges toward railing. DENISE rushes to him, wraps[2] his coat around him.)* Listen to me! I've lived here all my life, I know what winter's like! You Californians, you live in a dream land. *(JERRY fends her and the coat off[3]).*

JERRY: I've got to leave the coat here! It's got my name and address in it!

DENISE: Then you're serious about[4] this.

JERRY: You're damn right I'm serious about this!

DENISE: I'm so glad.

JERRY: (At rail) I've never been so serious about anything ... *(Doubletake[5])* What?

DENISE: The Sierra Club will really have some clout[6], once it gets a few members like you! *(JERRY starts to climb onto railing.)* Wait!

JERRY: What is it?

DENISE: You don't have to leave the whole coat with me! Just give me the slip of paper[7] ... *(Going through pockets, finds it.)* and put your coat back on.

JERRY: Oh. *(Gets down.)*

DENISE: You Californians! *(JERRY puts on coat. Starts for railing. Stops.)*

JERRY: No, I think I should take it off. *(Starts to take it off. Finds note he tore corner from. Reads it.)*

[1]**to put sb. in touch with** to help sb. to get in contact with – [2]**to wrap** to put sth. round an object – [3]**to fend sb./sth. off** to push sb./sth. away – [4]**to be serious about sth.** here: to want to do sth. – [5]**doubletake** reacting after a short delay – [6]**to have some clout** (col.) to get influence and power – [7]**a slip of paper** a small piece of paper

DENISE: Oh! Don't – read that ...

JERRY: *(Reads)* My sweetheart Harley ... *(Reads. Eyes wide. Closes note in embarrassment[1])*

DENISE: Pretty graphic[2], isn't it?

JERRY: Who's Harley?

DENISE: He was my husband. Until this morning.

JERRY: Did you get divorced[3] this morning?

DENISE: I found that note this morning.

JERRY: *(Reads, cautiously.)* "All my love, breathlessly, passionately[4] ..."

DENISE: Don't read the rest.

JERRY: "… LouEllen."

DENISE: Can you imagine? LouEllen? What kind of a name is LouEllen? From the East Coast, he says. Very sophisticated[5], he says. Very cosmopolitan[6], he says. Knows how to dress, he says. Knows what's happening, he says. Well, Jerry, I'll tell you, this gal[7] from Minnesota knows what's happening, you better believe me! She's only nineteen! But her make-up! Her clothes! She thinks she's living in Cosmo magazine, but I'll tell you where she's living –

JERRY: Harley ran off with –

DENISE: Don't speak her name!

JERRY: – What's her name.

DENISE: That's right.

JERRY: We've got a lot in common, I guess ...

DENISE: *(Ignoring him.)* But I'll tell you, Jerry with a J, he's not even worth the Sierra Club! If I'm not sophisticated enough for old Harley – what's wrong with my clothes? I've got to dress warm! I hope she freezes her little – off! *(JERRY, freezing, grabs his coat and puts it on.)* You poor goose, you're blue! Here, put on my coat. *(Takes off her coat – she has another on underneath it – and wraps it around JERRY,* despite his protests.)

JERRY: Please – no – really – Denise – *(Throws it at her.)* Don't! *(She's hurt.)* I appreciate[8] your concern[9] ... but it's ... too late. *(DENISE looks at JERRY's hands, ears, cheeks.)*

DENISE: Frostbite?

JERRY: Suicide[10].

V What does Jerry suddenly discover?

V How does Denise feel when she discovers that her husband has a girlfriend? (up to l. 185)

A What – up to this moment – has prevented Jerry from carrying out his plan to commit suicide[a]?

V What do you think will happen next?

[1]**embarrassment** a feeling of shyness and shame – [2]**graphic** very clear and detailed – [3]**to get divorced** to end a marriage by law – [4]**passionate** here: very strong (for feelings, esp. love) – [5]**sophisticated** knowing about culture, fashion and other socially important matters – [6]**cosmopolitan** having visited or lived in or knowing about a lot of different countries – [7]**gal** (colloquial) girl – [8]**to appreciate** here: to be grateful – [9]**concern** worry, care – [10]**suicide** the act of killing oneself

[a]**to commit suicide** to kill oneself

DENISE: I see. *(JERRY starts for railing. Takes off his coat.)* You Californians! Always exaggerating[1]! Minnesota winters are cold, but they're not that – *(JERRY on the railing, ready to jump.)* Jerry! *(Startled, JERRY starts to lose his balance. Tries to catch himself. Can't.) Jerry!* (DENISE rushes to him, catches him, pulls him back.) Jerry.

JERRY: Let me go, Denise. Tell her I hope she's happy with her damn lumberjack[2] –

DENISE: What are you doing, Jerry?

JERRY: She was happy enough with me when we lived in San Francisco – I'm a college professor –

DENISE: Oh, really?

JERRY: – and I was afraid she wouldn't like it here – she's used to warm weather, fresh fish, abalone[3] –

DENISE: What do you teach?

JERRY: – artichokes[4], avocados[5] – political science – the surf[6], Fisherman's Wharf[7] –

DENISE: Political science?

JERRY: But then, what does she do? She meets a lumberjack – runs off with him – cooks pancakes for him at a lumber camp[8] near the Boundary Waters – wherever they are – named Sven or Ole or Knut.

DENISE: Political science?

JERRY: So I'm doing the only thing I can do, Denise! Give me that coat! *(Grabs her coat, puts it on.)* And that one! *(JERRY pulls her next coat off of her, puts it on.)* And that! *(Muffler, hat, gloves, etc.)* And that!

DENISE: Jerry! Jerry!

JERRY: I'll sink for sure now! Straight to the bottom. Denise! They'll find my poor, bloated[9], waterlogged[10], drowned[11] body ... She'll be sorry! Even Sven will be sorry. Or Knut. *(Climbing onto railing.)*

DENISE: *(Calmly)* Jerry?

JERRY: Don't try to talk me out of it, Denise, my mind's made up.

DENISE: I really like that hat, Jerry. Would you mind leaving the hat?

JERRY: Oh. Of course. I'm sorry. *(Getting down, bringing her the hat.)* I was carried away[12].

DENISE: I understand.

JERRY: It was really thoughtless of me.

In what way does Denise's behaviour towards Jerry change?

What does Denise learn about Jerry's situation and his problem? (up to l. 228)

Fisherman's Wharf, Pier 39

Denise finally understands Jerry's intention. How does she now try to prevent him from killing himself (up to p. 34, l. 268)?

[1]**to exaggerate** to make sth. bigger, better, worse than it really is – [2]**lumberjack** a man whose job is to cut down trees – [3]**abalone** a big, edible mussel *(Seeohr)* – [4]**artichoke** ['a:titʃəʊk] – [5]**avocado** ['ævə'ka:dəʊ] – [6]**surf** white waves when they reach the beach – [7]**Fisherman's Wharf** a pier with shops, restaurants and video arcades in San Francisco – [8]**lumber camp** a camp where the lumberjacks live – [9]**bloated** swollen – [10]**waterlogged** full of water – [11]**to drown** if you cannot swim you will drown if you fall into water– [12]**to be carried away** to be so enthusiastic that you don't know when to stop

Golden Gate Bridge

DENISE: It's all right. You're under a lot of pressure[1].

JERRY: Yes. Yes, I am. *(Starts for railing, stops.)* You know, I've always admired people who could get involved politically. I just stand on the sidelines ... analyze ... observe ... the scientific approach[2] ... nonpartisan[3] ... objective *(Denise nods. JERRY reluctantly[4]* heads for railing.)

DENISE: You were planning on drowning?

JERRY: This is a bridge, isn't it? Boy, in San Francisco – the Golden Gate, the Bay Bridge, the San Rafael Bridge, the San Mateo ... Constant reminders[5] of the ultimate[6] choice! The fearful plunge[7], hundreds of feet into the dark, shark-infested[8] waters below ...

DENISE: *(Looking over the railing.)* It is dark.

JERRY: Well, it's night.

DENISE: Sharks?

JERRY: It's not a pretty death.

DENISE: *(Looking over railing.)* Maybe a few Northerns[9].

JERRY: Northerns?

DENISE: Northern pike[9]. *(Holds up her hands to indicate size.)* Under the ice. *(Jerry starts to jump.)*

JERRY: I'm not going to say goodbye, Denise. I don't like goodbyes. So ... Goodbye. *(Poised[10]. Stops. Doubletake.)* Ice?

DENISE: It's about two feet deep by now. *(JERRY gets carefully down.)*

> Why has Jerry not thought about this?

JERRY: That would hurt.

DENISE: You could aim for an ice fishing hole.

JERRY: I hadn't really paid any attention – I was so upset by the lumberjack – it got so cold so quickly – *(DENISE shivers.)* Oh, you're freezing! *(JERRY takes off coats, puts them on DENISE. They find themselves with their arms in the same coat. They laugh. They look into each other's eyes, grow serious.)*

> For the first time Jerry really pays attention to Denise and is concerned about her. Why is this an important moment for him and his relationship towards Denise?

DENISE: I know where we could get a cup of hot chocolate.

JERRY: *(Glances[11] at bridge railing.)* Well, I am pretty cold. I could probably think this through until spring ... *(The two of them walking off.)* Where is this place with the hot chocolate?

DENISE: My place.

THE END

[1]**pressure** *Druck* – [2]**the scientific approach** *der wissenschaftliche Ansatz* – [3]**nonpartisan** neutral – [4]**reluctant** unwilling – [5]**reminder** something that makes you remember – [6]**ultimate** final – [7]**plunge** jump – [8]**shark-infested** full of sharks – [9]**Northern/Northern pike** a fish *(Hecht)* – [10]**poised** balanced, ready to take action – [11]**to glance** to look at sth. very quickly

Focus on fictional characters

In a play, it is mostly what characters say themselves – or what other characters say about them – that reveals their **characteristic features** or **state of mind.** But the stage directions also help the reader, the actor and the audience to understand a character better.

Draw a chart and fill in what Jerry and Denise have in common and where they differ. Take into consideration both their words and the stage directions (for help see pp. 71ff.).

Jerry and Denise	**similarities**	**differences**
situation		
reaction to personal problems		
reaction to other people's problems		
general behaviour		
political views		
...		

With the help of your notes try to analyse the relationship between Jerry and Denise.

"All the world's a stage ...": Comedy

Although this play deals with a serious topic – suicide – the action does not turn into tragedy. Find out what makes this play so funny and enjoyable.

Writing options

1. Sum up the contents of the play in about ten sentences (for help see pp. 69f.).
2. The next morning, the local newspaper's front page reads like this: "Suicidal[1] Californian Saved By Courageous[2] Socialist!" Write an article for a tabloid (i. e. a popular paper) about the events on the bridge (for help see pp. 78f.).

An interview with William Borden

W. B. William Borden, author of *Jumping*

PAY Editors of *People Around You*

PAY First of all we'd like to thank you for giving permission to reprint your short play *Jumping* in our book.

W. B. My pleasure – I hope students in Germany like the play as much as they do in this country.

[1]**suicidal** wanting to kill yourself – [2]**courageous** brave

PAY Some of them don't find the play very easy but they all enjoy reading it. What we'd like to know is where you got the idea for *Jumping*.

W. B. In 1981 I was commissioned by the Playwrights' Center in Minneapolis to write a ten-minute play set in Minnesota. At first I wasn't sure what to write about. But the sight of an attempt at suicide, I knew, would be attention-getting; and, since I'm naturally inclined to see life's agonies through the lenses of comedy and absurdity, I knew that no one in the play would actually jump. As I was writing the play, I was thinking consciously of what it means to be a newcomer and of the stresses and opportunities that moving from one place to another create. But the details of the play came spontaneously as I was writing.

PAY Why did you add political motifs in the play?

W. B. I did this because I wanted to fill out the characters' personalities, contrasting Jerry's political passivity with Denise's practicality.

PAY Is it only seriousness that underlies the play then?

W. B. The political and personal issues are real. But, on the other hand, the play pokes fun at our inclination to take ourselves and our problems too seriously. Jerry, of course, doesn't really want to die; he wants attention and love. When Denise says politics gets her mind off personal problems, she offers sensible advice.

PAY Why did you set the scene on a bridge?

W. B. Bridges are both connecting and dividing, the sites of despair as well as new beginnings. In Minneapolis, bridges span the Mississippi to connect that city with St. Paul.

PAY You have just said that you didn't really know what to write about when you started.

W. B. That's true. The details of the play came spontaneously as I was writing it. When I began writing, Jerry was ready to jump and Denise came on the scene, but I didn't know what would happen next, nor did I know, until I wrote Jerry's lines, why he was distraught. Nor did I know how the play would end until I got to the end, when the realization came to me that, of course, the river was frozen.

PAY So you did not plan the play before you wrote it.

W. B. I had been thinking about a variety of things, but I did not outline the play before I wrote it.

PAY Well, it was very interesting for us to visit an author's workshop. Thank you very much for this interview.

William Borden

Look up the words you don't know in your English dictionary.

Project The Split Decision – Writing and Acting

The following text is the beginning of a short play by William Moseley. Read it carefully and make sure that you understand where and when it takes place, who the characters are, what they talk about and where the basic conflict may lie. Working in pairs or in small groups continue the dialogue: How will the conversation between Ginger and David go on? How will they behave (stage directions)? What will happen at the climax? How will the play end?
If you look again at the stage directions you will see that not many props are needed. So you may try to act your play out in front of your class or even in front of the whole school???

Characters: David – in his twenties
Ginger – in her twenties

Setting: The living room of Ginger and David's apartment. One half of the room is ***hers****. Its low, comfortable sofa, [...] soft drapes, and throw rugs give it a warm, home-like atmosphere. The other half of the room is* ***his****. [...] Its steel desk with a home computer, its tile floor without carpets, and its chrome and plastic furniture, [...] create an effect of cold practicality and efficiency.*

At Rise: Lights up on DAVID, seated at his desk, facing the audience, typing at the keyboard of his computer. After a few moments, GINGER enters, carrying a serving tray with coffee pot, cups, saucers, and spoons. She stops unhappily when she sees DAVID working. Then she crosses to set the tray on the coffee table in front of the couch.

David: (Hearing the dishes rattle, but not looking up.) Ginger –?

Ginger: (Only half serious.) Know what, David? Some evening you're going to be all absorbed in that machine, and call out "Ginger?" – and it *won't* be me.

David: (Barely listening, continuing to work). Hmm? And who'll it be?

Ginger: Oh ... maybe nobody.

David: Yeah, well – Have to put this in memory, so I can boot it up for Harris tomorrow morning.

Ginger: You *gave* me a full report – all through dinner. While *I* was hoping we'd have time to talk about – [...]

Unit 3 Paths to Peace

Getting into the Unit

Look at this collage made of a cartoon and some quotations and sayings and talk about your first impressions.

A weapon is an enemy even to its owner.

One thousand friends is too little, one enemy is too much.

Nothing to kill or die for ...

War is a game played by old men who have lost interest in life.

Death came out of the sky in the bright afternoon ...

Decide to be peaceful ...

I seek strength ... to be able to fight my greatest enemy, myself.

Pile the bodies high at Austerlitz and Waterloo ...

Respect for the rights of another, that is peace.

He has died for those oppressed ...

Joy is the daughter of peace.

He is the universal soldier and he really is to blame ...

When you now read the following poems you will find some of these quotations.

Poetry

A **poem** is a special form of literature. It is arranged in lines so that a certain rhythm is created. Traditional poems use **metre** (cf. p. 42) and contain **rhyming words** whereas modern poems are often written in **free verse** (cf. p. 44). A poem may consist of one or several **stanzas** (cf. p. 40). The poet chooses the words in the poem for their sound and special meanings and combines them in unusual ways to create **images** (cf. p. 42) which stimulate the reader's imagination.

The Ballad of the Green Berets

Barry Sadler, Robin Moore

Before you read the text, have a look at this picture:

What do you think the insignia[a] on the soldier's uniform mean?

Fighting soldiers from the sky,
Fearless men who jump and die,
Men who mean just what they say,
The brave men of The Green Beret.

Silver wings[1] upon their chests[2],
These are men, America's best.
One hundred men we'll test today
But only three win The Green Beret.

Trained to live off nature's land,
Trained to combat[3], hand to hand.
Men who fight by night and day,
Courage take from The Green Beret.

Silver wings upon their chests,
These are men, America's best.
One hundred men we'll test today
But only three win The Green Beret.

Back at home a young wife waits,
Her Green Beret has met his fate.
He has died for those oppressed[4],
Leaving her this last request[5].

Put silver wings on my son's chest,
Make him one of America's best.
He'll be a man they'll test one day,
Have him win The Green Beret.

[1]**wing** *Flügel* – [2]**chest** the upper front part of the body – [3]**to combat** to fight – [4]**to oppress** to cause to feel ill or sad – [5]**request** a polite demand

[a]**insignia** a sign that shows that a person belongs to a particular organization

A closer look at the text:

1. What kind of men are presented in ll. 1–16?
2. Look again at ll. 17–24: What has happened to one of the soldiers? What is his last wish?

What do you think?

1. What impression do you get of the soldiers in this poem?
2. What kind of attitude towards war does the poem reveal?
3. Would you fulfil the soldier's last wish in ll. 21–24?

A special type of poem

A **ballad** is a poem or a song that tells a story. It often has a noble or tragic tone.

Try to explain why this poem can be called a ballad.

The poem and its structure

A **stanza** is a group of lines that form a unit in a poem. The repetition of some lines or a complete stanza is called a **refrain.**

"The Ballad of the Green Berets" is divided into six stanzas. Try to analyse the poem's structure by explaining the meaning and function of each stanza.

The poem's rhyme

Rhyme is the repetition of sounds at the end of two or more words – as in "one" and "sun" or "higher" and "desire".
The rhyme may be at the end or in the middle of a poem's lines. Typical **rhyme schemes** are rhyming couplets (aabbcc...), alternate rhyme (ababcdcd...) or enclosed rhyme (abbacddc...). Rhyme creates a link between words or ideas.

Write down the rhyme scheme of "The Ballad of the Green Berets". With the help of two or three examples try to explain why the poet makes certain words rhyme. Does anything strike you as unusual?

Up to you

Try to write an anti-poem which shows the horrors of war. If you want to you may choose to keep the form of "The Ballad of the Green Berets". You could start like this:

Trembling soldiers from the sky,
Frightened men who jump and die,
...

The Children William Soutar

Before you read the poem:

This is an excerpt from a newspaper article on the war in Vietnam:

"... Over the radio, the impersonal voice of a SAC ground controller announced 'seven minutes to 'hack'[1] (bomb release point)'. The count droned on until hack, when Harris punched[2] a black button and 30 tons of high explosives cascaded toward the ground more than 30,000 feet below us. There was no shock, no noise, no sight of explosions. Only the impersonal voice of the controller: 'Bombs in the target area[3]. That was a good run, fellows. Have a nice ride home and see you another day.' ... In a small oven in the cockpit the men began heating TV dinners. They had not seen their target, their enemy, or the effect of their mission."
(Time, August 2, 1968.)

A What is your impression of modern warfare?

The poem *The Children* shows what the soldiers in their bomber do not see.

Upon the street they lie
Beside the broken stone:
The blood of children stares from the broken stone.

Death came out of the sky
In the bright afternoon:
Darkness slanted over[4] the bright afternoon.

Again the sky is clear
But upon earth a stain[5]:
The earth is darkened with a darkening stain.

A wound which everywhere
Corrupts[6] the hearts of men:
The blood of children corrupts the hearts of men.

Silence is in the air:
The stars move to their places:
Silent and serene[7] the stars move to their places.

But from the earth the children stare
With blind and fearful faces:
And our charity[8] is in the children's faces.

A **A closer look at the text**:
Try to describe in your own words the event which is dealt with in the poem.

[1]**hack** bomb release point – [2]**to punch** here: to press – [3]**target area** *Zielbereich* – [4]**to slant over** *sich neigen über* – [5]**stain** dirty patch of colour – [6]**to corrupt** to cause to change from good to bad – [7]**serene** calm and peaceful – [8]**charity** sympathy and kindness

What do you think?

1. The poem shows the results of a bomb attack. How do you feel when you read this text?
2. The newspaper article and the poem both describe a bomb attack. Can you try to explain the differences between the two texts?

The world of the imagination: Figurative language

Images (similes, metaphors or **symbols**) are examples of **figurative language**. The words that are used in figurative language mean more than their usual definition in a dictionary. By using figurative language the author creates special meanings or effects.
A **metaphor** is an indirect comparison. A comparison says that one thing is *like* another; the metaphor says that one thing *is* another. In order to understand a metaphor you must find the "link" between the two objects or ideas, e.g. "My love is a red rose", "the sands of time", "crocodile tears", etc.
A **simile** is a comparison between different things. It is indicated by "like" or "as", e.g. "Her lips are as red as roses."
A **symbol** is an object that stands for some abstract idea, e.g. the cross for Christianity or the rose for love.

Which forms of figurative language can you find in this poem? Choose one example for each form and try to explain its meaning within the poem and its effect on the reader.

Metre

Metre is the pattern of stressed and unstressed syllables within a line of a poem. The type of metre chosen by the poet gives the poem a certain rhythm and stresses important key-words or ideas. It also helps the reader to memorize the poem.
In traditional poetry, this pattern is regular, for example:
◡ ' (iambic metre) ; ' ◡ (trochee) ; ◡ ◡ ' (anapaest) ; ' ◡ ◡ (dactyl) ; ' ' (spondee)

1. Read the poem aloud and pay attention to the way stressed and unstressed syllables follow each other.
2. Then copy the first stanza and mark its lines to show the metre. The first line of "The Children" can be transcribed like this:

   ◡ / ◡ / ◡ /
   Upon the street they lie ...
3. Now do the same with the second stanza. Can you explain the effect of the change in metre?
4. As you continue with this task, try to show the extent to which the metre chosen by the poet reinforces or affects the meaning of the poem.

Writing option

Write a newspaper article that reports on the bomb attack which is dealt with in the poem (for help see pp. 78f.).

Grass Carl Sandburg

Here is some information before you read the poem:

In this text some places where famous battles were fought are mentioned. At Austerlitz and Waterloo two 19th century battles were fought by Napoleon. He won the Battle of Austerlitz on December 2nd, 1805, but at the Battle of Waterloo on June 18th, 1815, he was decisively[1] defeated by combined Prussian, English and Dutch forces, losing nearly all his soldiers. The expression "to meet one's Waterloo" is still used today.
The Battle of Gettysburg, fought from July 1st-3rd, 1863, marked a decisive turning point in the American Civil War. The Allied Forces of the North won this battle, in which there were about 40,000 casualties[2].
The First World War battles at Ypres (Belgium) and Verdun (France) were typical of the very heavy losses suffered in trench warfare[3]. In the Battle of Verdun, for example, which was fought between French and German troops in 1916, 714,000 soldiers lost their lives.

[1]**decisive** unquestionable – [2]**casualty** a person who is killed or wounded in war – [3]**trench warfare** *Stellungskrieg*

Fill in the gaps

In the poem some words have been left out. Below each stanza you will find a list of words that may fit into the gaps. Choose the words that **you** think are missing and try to justify your choices when presenting your ideas to the class.

Grass

1.
Pile the ________ high at Austerlitz and Waterloo.
________ them under and let me ____________ .
I am the ______________ ; I cover all.

dig – grass – work – dead – sleep – bodies – shovel – grave-digger

2.
And pile them high at Gettysburg –
And pile them high at Ypres and Verdun.
________ them under and let me ___________.
Two years, ten years, and _________ ask the ____________ :
What ______________ is this?
Where are we now?
I am the _______________.
Let me ________________.

passengers – place – work – tourists – grass – cemetery – sleep – conductor – sleep – dig – grave-digger – shovel – work – guide

What do you think?

1. Compare your ideas with the poet's choice of words: To what extent does the effect on the reader change, depending on the words that are chosen?
2. Why do you think the poet has chosen the battles mentioned in the poem?
3. What may be the message of the poem?

The speaker

The speaker in a fictional text is a person invented by the author – and usually not identical with him or her – who seems to talk directly to the reader and present the text to him or her.

Why does the poet choose the grass as the speaker of this poem? Try to explain the effect this choice has on the reader.

A look at poetic form: Free verse

The poem "Grass" shows no consistent rhyme or metre. This type of poetry is called **free verse.** Try to explain why it can still be called a poem.

O Great Spirit Tom Whitecloud

A
I seek strength,
Not to be superior[1] to my brothers
But to be able to fight
My greatest enemy, myself.

B
Make me wise, so that I may know
The things you have taught my people,
The lessons you have hidden
In every leaf and rock.

C
Make me ever ready to come to you,
With clean hands and straight eye,
So when life fades[2] as the fading sunset
My spirit may come to you without shame.

D
Let me walk in beauty.
And make my eyes ever behold[3]
The red and purple sunset.
Make my hands respect
The things you have made,
My ears sharp to hear your voice.

E
Whose voice I hear in the winds
And whose breath gives life
To all the world,
Hear me. I am a man before you.
One of your many children.
I am small and weak.
I need your strength and wisdom[4].

The stanzas of this poem have been mixed up. Can you put them in the right order?

If you are not sure about your ideas, here are some questions which may help you to find the correct order:

1. Who is the "I" in the poem?
2. Who is the "you"?
3. Can C be the opening or closing stanza? Why (not)?
4. Can E be the opening or closing stanza? Why (not)?
5. Which sequence is more likely – A B D – B D A – D A B – D B A? Why?

When you have established what you think is the correct order, try to give a one-sentence summary of each stanza. Is there some kind of logical development within the poem?

What do you think?

1. Can you characterize the speaker's relationship to nature?
2. Why does he pray for the strength to fight himself? (cf. ll. 1–4)
3. What kind of peace does the speaker wish to achieve?

A prayer – and a poem

Try to find out which elements in this text (ideas and/or words) show that it is both a prayer and a poem.

Up to you

With a partner or in small groups discuss possible ways of solving conflicts without using violence, and finding inner peace as well. Use a mind map (cf. p. 25) to organise your ideas, and then present them to the class for further discussion.

[1]**superior** better than – [2]**to fade** to lose strength – [3]**to behold** to notice, to see – [4]**wisdom** *Weisheit*

Imagine John Lennon

Before you read the text:

In an interview in 1971 John Lennon said about this song: "... the song is like a child's song. I wanted to keep it that a child could understand it."

When you read the text try to keep these words in mind.

Imagine there's no heaven, it's easy if you try,
no hell below us, above us only sky.
Imagine all the people living for today.

You may say I'm a dreamer, but I'm not the only one,
I hope some day you'll join us, and the world will be as one.

Imagine there's no countries, it isn't hard to do;
nothing to kill or die for, and no religion too.
Imagine all the people living life in peace.

You may say I'm a dreamer, but I'm not the only one,
I hope some day you'll join us, and the world will be as one.

Imagine no possessions, I wonder if you can.
No need for greed[1] or hunger, a brotherhood[2] of man.
Imagine all the people sharing all the world.

You may say I'm a dreamer, but I'm not the only one,
I hope some day you'll join us, and the world will be as one.

A closer look at the song:

1. What areas of life does the speaker talk about in ll. 1–8?
2. Look again at ll. 11–15: How should people behave towards each other and what is the speaker's hope?

[1]**greed** strong desire for more food, wealth, etc. – [2]**brotherhood** the quality or state of being brothers

possession - Besitztum
greed - Gier / Begierde

The song's message

1. Do you think that the speaker is just "a dreamer" (ll. 4, 9, 14)?
2. Is the song really "a child's song"? (cf. the pre-reading assignment)

The choice of words

The **choice of words** made by the author influences the reader in different ways.

In "Imagine" John Lennon uses some words that make the reader think about various reasons for wars to start. The words that he uses stand for different concepts, ideas, or even ideologies.

1. Read the song again and try to fill in a chart like this one:

line(s)	words in the text	what they stand for
l. 1	heaven	paradise, religion, the promise of a better life after death, ...
l. 2	hell	death, sin, punishment, religion, ...
l. 2	sky	nature, weather, freedom, ...
l. 6	...	...

2. With the help of this chart explain some of the factors which cause wars to break out.
3. How – according to the speaker – may wars be prevented and a "brotherhood of man" achieved?

Repetition and variation

In poetry, especially in ballads or songs, the refrain helps to structure the text and makes the reader or listener remember the message. Sometimes these repetitions are slightly altered to avoid monotony or help to keep the reader's or listener's attention.

Find out where in "Imagine" John Lennon uses repetition and/or variation and analyse the effect of these stylistic devices.

Writing option

Add one or more stanzas to the song: Think of more ways of preventing or stopping wars, and try to keep the pattern of the song.

Comparing two poems

Here is another poem that appeals to the reader to work for lasting peace in the world. Read it carefully and try to find out what the two poems have in common and where they differ. Think about what is said in the text, how the poem is structured and which words the poet has chosen to drive his message home to the reader (for help see pp. 79f.).

Decide to be peaceful
Render[1] others peaceful
Be a model of peace
Irradiate[2] your peace
Love passionately the peace
of our beautiful planet
Do not listen to the warmongers[3],
hateseeders[4] and powerseekers
Dream always of a peaceful,
warless, disarmed[5] world
Think always of a peaceful world
Work always for a peaceful world
Switch on and keep on, in yourself,
the peaceful buttons,
those marked love,
serenity, happiness, truth,
kindness, friendliness,
understanding and tolerance
Pray and thank God every day
for peace
Pray for the United Nations
and all peacemakers
Pray for the leaders of nations
who hold the peace of the world
in their hands
Pray God to let our planet at long last
become the Planet of Peace
And sing in unison[6] with all humanity[7]:
"Let there be peace on Earth
And let it begin with me."

Robert Muller

Do you remember what John Lennon said about the song "Imagine"? (cf. p. 46). Which of the two texts do you think is easier to understand?

[1]**to render** to cause to be – [2]**to irradiate** *ausstrahlen* – [3]**warmonger** a person who tries to cause a war – [4]**hateseeder** *Hassverbreiter* – [5]**to disarm** to take weapons away from sb. – [6]**in unison** together – [7]**humanity** human beings generally

Project Write and Design

Make a poster or a collage which is intended to persuade people to work for peace or stop wars. You can use words, sentences or even stanzas taken from texts that you have studied, or write your own texts and combine them with clippings from papers or your own drawings.

Unit 4 Boston – Today and Yesterday

Getting into the Unit

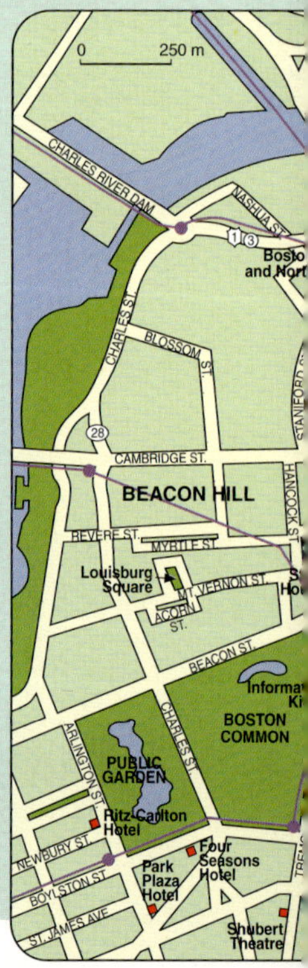

Boston is the capital and largest city of Massachusetts, one of the New England States. With its 695,000 people it ranks 13th in population of American Cities, but when the Metropolitan areas are considered, Boston is regarded as the 6th largest city in the US. It was founded in 1630; the first people who settled in Boston in the seventeenth and eighteenth centuries were British. Today you will find here – as in other big cities – people from all over the world. Boston is a fascinating mixture of everything old and new in an American metropolis. Its magnificent skyscrapers form pleasing backgrounds to old colonial brick houses. What makes Boston unique is that historical sites and national landmarks, examples of Boston's historic past, are located side-by-side with business buildings, hotels, and residential neighborhoods.

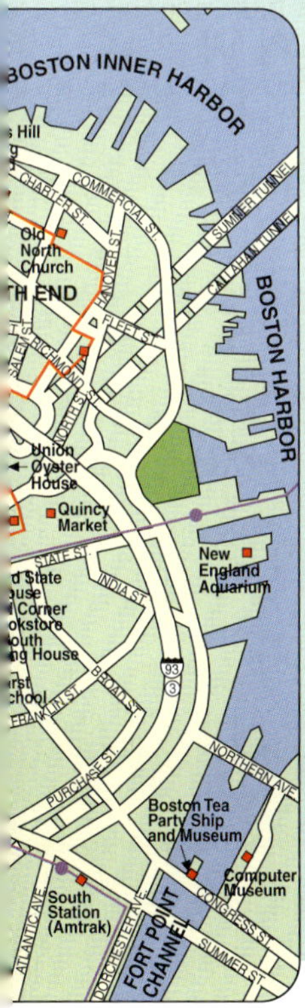

Boston's famous firsts

1634 The first public park in America is established (Boston Common).
1635 The first public school, Boston Latin School, is founded.
1636 The first American College, Harvard is founded in Cambridge.
1639 The first American Post Office opens in Boston.
1653 The first public library opens in Boston.
1716 The first American Lighthouse is built in Boston Harbor.
1775 The first battle of The Revolution is fought near Boston.
1845 The first sewing machine is invented by Elias Howe in Boston.
1872 The first adding machine to print totals is patented in Boston.
1875 The first Christmas Cards are published in Boston.
1875 The first Baseball glove is worn by C. C. Waite in Boston.
1897 The first Annual Marathon Race in America is started in Boston.
1898 The first Subway system in America is opened in Boston.
1900 The first Davis Cup Tennis matches are held in Boston.
1928 The first Computer is developed at M. I. T.

What information about Boston do you get from this collage?
Copy this chart and fill it in.

location	history	buildings	population	importance	…

Non-fictional texts
In this Unit, you will get to know various kinds of non-fictional texts. A non-fictional text (e. g. a newspaper report, a letter, etc.) is based on facts whereas a fictional text (e. g. a short story) does not deal with real events or real people.

Boston's Layout: Downtown, Neighborhoods, Suburbs

Downtown

Downtown with all its narrow streets is the heart of the city of Boston. This area lies between the City Hall and Chinatown. The City Hall, a very modern building, is located in the new part of the city where you will find most of the office buildings and banks. Chinatown gives a colorful picture of Chinese restaurants and shops. In Downtown there are lots of department stores, one of them is Filene's. The store is known for its basement, where everything is automatically reduced in price according to how many days it has been in the store. In Downtown you also find Boston's three Shopping Malls, e. g. the one at Quincy Market. The Shopping Mall is an American institution. It is a place where Americans of all ages spend a lot of time not only shopping but also meeting friends and hanging out. The first Mall was opened outside Seattle in 1950. One of the attractions in Boston Downtown is the "Freedom Trail" (see p. 61). Boston is known for a lot of famous restaurants and pubs, e. g. the Union Oyster House, the oldest restaurant in America, and the Bull & Finch Pub, the place where the wellknown TV series "Cheers" was produced.

Downtown is the central part of any American city with banks, shops and government buildings.

A **description** is an objective representation of things, persons, actions, etc., here of a city, without any personal comments.

Sum up the information about Boston's Downtown.

Neighborhoods

As in other big cities it is not Downtown which makes the city but its neighborhoods. Neighborhoods are districts round the center. Most of Boston's 16 neighborhoods are located south of central Boston. The map shows that some of them, e. g. West Roxbury or Hyde Park, are rather far from Downtown. People here identify themselves as coming from these neighborhoods and not from Boston itself.

Suburbs

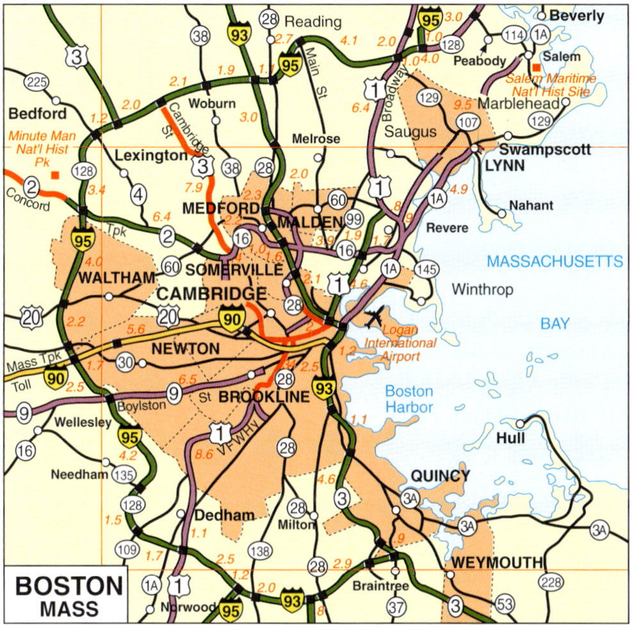

Suburbs are not the same as "Vororte" of German towns but separate new towns located round a city. The city and the suburbs form the metropolitan area.

For some time people have thought that living in the center of a big city is less attractive than living in the green suburbs[1]. So the rich have left the city. A lot of freeways[2] have helped this trend. In suburbs people find both the peacefulness[3] of the countryside and the activity of life in the city. Suburbs are now part of an American city. As rings of suburbs have become wider and wider, cities' metropolitan areas are now enormous.

Around the city of Boston you will find 76 separate cities and towns. Now more than three million people live in Metropolitan or Greater Boston so that Boston is regarded as the 6th largest city in the United States.

Suburbanization[4] has had a lot of consequences. The city slums[5], where the rent for old houses is cheaper, are populated[6] by those who do not have the money to move into suburbs: the uneducated[7], the unskilled[8], the unemployed[9]. Social problems such as crime are the result. But it was not only the people who moved out into suburbs, industry followed. So the yield of taxes[10] went down and cities were led into financial problems which are very difficult to solve.

While you read this text note down all the information about suburbs:

people	
population	
problems	

What could cities do to improve the living conditions in city centers?

[1]**suburb** here: town outside the city – [2]**freeway** (AE) motorway – [3]**peacefulness** quietness – [4]**suburbanization** building more and more suburbs – [5]**slum** a dirty, crowded and poor part of a town – [6]**to populate** to inhabit, to form the population of – [7]**uneducated** not educated – [8]**unskilled** not specially trained for a job – [9]**unemployed** without work – [10]**yield of taxes** *Steueraufkommen*

Aspects of Life in Boston

Restaurants and pubs

There are many fine restaurants and pubs in Boston, among them the Union Oyster House, the oldest restaurant in continuous service in the United States and the famous Bull & Finch Pub, the place where the TV series "Cheers" was produced. Nearly everybody visiting Boston goes and sees this pub.

Only in Boston you can see the "opening shot"[1] of "Cheers"[2]. Filmed in Hollywood, the show is based on the one-and-only Bull & Finch Pub.

Hollywood may have Sam Malone, but only Boston has the Bull & Finch Pub.

Cheers®

Only in Boston can you eat on the "set"[3]. The Bull & Finch Pub, inspiration[4] for the setting[5] of "Cheers", serves sensational pub food & drink daily. Our Bloody Mary[6] has been toasted[7] the "Best in Boston".

Owner Tom Kershaw invites you to enjoy the "Cheers Experience"[8] in Boston.

Tell your friends all the "secrets[9]" behind "Cheers". Come to the original place where "everybody knows your name" – the Bull & Finch Pub!

BULL & FINCH PUB®

Only in Boston can you walk away from the Pub with an official "Cheers" souvenir.

Open Daily 11 a.m.-2 a.m.
84 Beacon Street
across from the Public Garden
Beacon Hill, Boston
617/227-9605

[1]**opening shot** first pictures in a film production – [2]**"Cheers"** name of a TV series – [3]**set** the scenery for a film – [4]**inspiration** idea – [5]**setting** place where an event takes place (here: where "Cheers" was produced) – [6]**Bloody Mary** alcoholic drink: tomato juice & vodka – [7]**to be toasted** here: praised as – [8]**Cheers experience** "Cheers" – *Erlebnis* – [9]**secret** sth. that you do not tell other people

An **advertisement** or ad is a notice in a newspaper, on a wall, on TV, etc. It tries to persuade the reader to do or buy something. The usual elements are: headline, body copy (text) and pictures.

Let's have a look at the ad "Cheers" which can be found in the Boston Guest Quick Guide.

Headline

There are actually two headlines. What is striking about them? What effect are they intended to have on the reader?

Body copy

This advertisement does not consist of one piece of body copy only but of several texts right through the ad. What do you learn about the pub, and what is missing? Take notes.

What the pub offers:
What it promises:
What you would like to know:

Illustrations

Explain the effect of the illustrations in the ad.

Language

In advertisements colloquial, sometimes even incorrect language is used. What sort of language is used here, and what mood is created?

What about you?

Imagine you will be in Boston one day. Would this ad persuade you to go to the Bull & Finch Pub? – Why – why not?

Educational institutions and their problems

Boston has always played a very important role in education. There are 32 Colleges and Universities in the City, among them Harvard University, the country's oldest and one of the most famous institutions of higher learning, founded in 1636. And it was in Boston that the first public high school was established[1] in the same year. Today there are about 110 schools in Boston with around 60,000 students. The city of-

✓ Read this text carefully and do task 1 afterwards.

[1]**to establish** to found

fers a strong educational program for young people from every social, ethnic and economic background. A typical class tends to be 1% Native American, 11% Asian, 20% Hispanic, 23% White and 45% Black. As it is rather difficult to teach pupils from different nations in one class bilingual[1] programs have been started.

A serious[2] problem in the US in general is school attendance[3]. In Boston, students have to be in school at least 85 per cent of the school term[4] in order to get a passing mark. That makes students go to school more regularly. Furthermore Boston has, as many big cities, the so-called computerized telephone called the "Robot". Students' parents are telephoned all day long. The parents get a computerized telephone call which tells them that their child is not in school and asks them to call back, and that works quite well.

Another interesting point is safety[5] in schools. Big cities have metal detectors in their schools to check[6] students for weapons when they arrive in the morning. Boston has two such metal detectors. All the other schools rely on[7] teachers and aides[8] who are there on patrol. This is very important because students bring guns and knives to school. Fortunately they use them very rarely[9] in class. In the past it happened only once that a student was killed with a gun. But, of course, a lot of fights go on in schools. That is why there are policemen in school buildings, so-called security guards[10], who work for the city. Since they do not have the same power that a regular police officer has, they have to call the Boston police to come in to arrest somebody when there is a serious problem.

About the text

1. Note down all the items about schools dealt with in the text:

schools	students	school attendance	safety

2. Pick out one aspect, please, and comment on it (for help see pp. 73f.).
3. Can you think of other problems a school has to cope[11] with?

[1]**bilingual** speaking two languages – [2]**serious** *ernst* – [3]**school attendance** being in school – [4]**term** part of the school year, usually five months – [5]**safety** opposite of danger – [6]**to check** here: to search – [7]**to rely on** *sich verlassen auf* – [8]**aide** a person who helps – [9]**rarely** not often – [10]**security guard** *Sicherheitsposten* – [11]**to cope with** to succeed in dealing with a difficult problem

Another common problem is alcohol use. Duxbury High School's approach to this problem is described in the following newspaper report.

In Duxbury High test, subject[1] is alcohol use

'It's a beautiful deterrent[2]. Kids know that no matter how much gum they have in their mouths, they can't fool the breath test.'

WAYNE OGDEN, Duxbury High principal

By Bob Hohler
GLOBE STAFF

In an uncommon[3] approach[4] to a common problem, Duxbury High School has a new plan to combat[5] student drinking: an alcohol breath test[6].

School officials launched[7] the initiative[8] after several Duxbury students were arrested at the first two football games of the season on charges of[9] disorderly conduct[10] and possession[11] of alcohol.

Duxbury appears to be the second Massachusetts community[12] to employ[13] the test. In nearby Rockland, the high school has been using it for more than a year, and officials find the threat[14] of the test has deterred student drinking.

Under the plan, officials will administer the test[15] to students they suspect[16] have consumed alcohol[17]. Students who flunk the test[18] will be turned over to their parents or police, according to the policy.

"If it saves[19] one accident where someone is hurt or killed, then it will be worth the grief[20] we may get for doing it," said Wayne Ogden, the high school principal[21].

In an extraordinary[22] series of tragedies, six Duxbury students died in alcohol-related accidents[23] in the mid-1980s. The schools responded[24] by expanding[25] alcohol education programs, including a peer project in which high school students explore the issue with seventh and eighth graders[26].

But the arrests at the football games indicate[27] that problems persist[28], Ogden said. As a result, he opted[29] for the breath test, which he had used the previous[30] five years as a high school principal in Springfield, Vt.

"It's a beautiful deterrent," he said. "Kids know that no matter how much gum they have in their mouths, they can't fool[31] the breath test."

Several Vermont schools use the test, but authorities said they believed Rockland was the only other Massachusetts school. No Rockland student has been disciplined[32] after taking the test, said A. Scott MacKinlay, the Rockland High principal.

[1]**subject** *Thema* – [2]**deterrent** *Abschreckung* – [3]**uncommon** unusual – [4]**approach** way, step – [5]**to combat** to fight – [6]**alcohol breath test** (e.g. an alcohol breath test shows how much alcohol sb. has drunk) – [7]**to launch** to start – [8]**initiative** first step – [9]**on the charge of** (e.g. he was arrested on the charge of murder) – [10]**disorderly conduct** bad behaviour – [11]**possession** having something – [12]**community** group of people who live together – [13]**to employ** here: to use – [14]**threat** *Drohung* – [15]**to administer a test** to apply/to use a test – [16]**to suspect** to have the feeling that a person may have done sth. wrong – [17]**to consume alcohol** to drink alcohol – [18]**to flunk the test** (inf.) not to pass the test – [19]**to save** to make sth. unnecessary – [20]**grief** sorrow – [21]**principal** (AE) headmaster of a school – [22]**extraordinary** not usual – [23]**alcohol-related accident** an accident caused by alcohol – [24]**to respond** to react – [25]**to expand** to make larger – [26]**peer project in which high school students explore the issue with seventh and eighth graders** *Projekt, bei dem High-School-Studenten das Problem mit Schülern der siebten und achten Klasse erörtern* – [27]**to indicate** to show – [28]**to persist** to continue to exist – [29]**to opt for** to decide for – [30]**previous** earlier in time – [31]**to fool** to deceive – [32]**to discipline** to punish

The Boston Globe and *The Boston Herald* are the city's newspapers. Read the headline and the quotation[1] first. What do they reveal about the content of the article?

In a **report** the writer informs the reader objectively about events which can be easily checked by others. He does not give his personal view of the events. A report consists of a headline, lead (introduction with the most important information) and body (facts reported in greater detail).
A text form variant of the report is the news story.

Enter your findings in a chart like this:

who
does what
where
when
and why

A report answers the five w's, the who, what, where, when and also the why and how questions. As you read this report find out: who does what, where, when and why?

And your opinion?
Do you think the alcohol test is a good thing?

Boston: the Cradle of the United States

The way to the Boston Tea Party

The English colonies in North America were separate communities scattered[2] along the Atlantic coast from New England to Georgia. Each colony was governed by a very powerful governor who represented the king of England. The governors carried out the policies and enforced[3] the laws

A **historical report** is an objective description of events in the past.

[1]**quotation** words that sb. has written or said – [2]**to scatter** to spread over a wide area – [3]**to enforce a law** to make people obey a law

of England. As a lot of money was needed to run the colonies, Parliament raised heavy taxes. The people in Boston and in the colonies immediately resented[1] these laws. And when several thousand Redcoats (British soldiers) were suddenly quartered[2] in Boston, serious trouble erupted. "No Taxation without Representation" became the hue and cry[3] in Boston. On the night of March 5, 1770 British soldiers fired into a rioting[4] crowd. This event was later called the "Boston Massacre". The unrest reached its climax when King George of England imposed[5] a tax upon tea.

What do you think is meant by "No Taxation without Representation"?

The Tea Party and its consequences

When in November 1773, three ships were arriving in Boston Harbor public protest rose to new heights. There were posters all over the town.

As the ships remained unloaded, the Governor of Massachusetts stationed two warships off the coast. The citizens of Boston responded[6] by holding a mass meeting at the Old South Church on December 16, 1773. At the same time a much smaller meeting was taking place in a printing shop: Boston's Sons of Liberty were disguising[7] themselves as "Mohawk" Indians, complete with feathers, warpaint and tomahawks. In the early evening the Mohawks went on the "warpath", leading the crowd down to where the ships lay. The eighty men boarded the tea ships and in less than three hours destroyed all 342 tea chests or threw them into the sea.

No Taxation without Representation!

Down with the Tea Tax!

Nobody shall buy tea until we're free!

Throw the tea into the sea!

The Tea Party, as this event was later called, was the beginning of the end for England in America.

When the news of the Boston Tea Party reached the ears of the king, he punished the population of Boston by repressive[8] measures. He passed the so-called Intolerable Acts, e.g. the Boston Port Act, which provided[9] that no ship could enter or leave Boston harbor until the town had paid for the tea. The Acts aroused enormous opposition in Boston and elsewhere.

[1]**to resent the law** to feel angry about the law – [2]**to quarter** to put so. in a particular place – [3]**hue and cry** angry protest abouth sth. – [4]**to riot** to behave in a violent way – [5]**to impose a tax upon sth.** to order that sth. should be taxed – [6]**to respond** to answer – [7]**to disguise** to change someone's appearance – [8]**repressive** severe and cruel – [9]**to provide** here: to state that sth. must happen

Lexington...

(The scenes of the first clash of arms in the American Revolution)

... and Concord

The hatred of the Intolerable Act had turned Boston into an armed camp. An English regiment of Redcoats, as the British soldiers were called, was patrolling the town in and outside Boston. American Patriots began to form militia companies. On the night of April 18, 1775 the Redcoats were preparing to march out and capture weapons that the Patriots had hidden at Lexington, a village not far from Boston. On April 19, the first shot was fired near Lexington, "the shot heard round the world". This clash of arms was followed by a fight at Concord's North Bridge: The war for American Independence had begun.

The Battle of Bunker Hill

Two months later, the first real battle of the War was fought. The Americans had occupied Bunker Hill and Breed's Hill, two high points across the harbor of Boston. Working all night, they built an earthen fort on top of the hill, a good position to fight British warships in the harbor. Could the Americans mount heavy cannon on that hill Boston Harbor would be untenable[1]. But the British reacted immediately. 2,200 men under General Howe moved across the Charles River to the peninsula[2] and attacked the Americans who finally lost the battle on June 17, 1775.

The Declaration of Independence

In May 1776, a month after the military actions at Lexington and Concord, the Second Continental Congress met in Philadelphia with John Hancock from Boston as its President. Congress declared the 13 American colonies to be free and independent of Britain. A congressional committee drew up a Declaration of Independence which was signed on July 4, 1776 by John Hancock and 55 other representatives.

Can you summarize what you have learned about Boston's role in American history (pp. 58ff.)? For help see Writer's Workshop pp. 69f.

[1]**untenable** impossible to defend – [2]**peninsula** a piece of land almost completely surrounded by water but joined to land

The Freedom Trail – the bridge between today and yesterday

The Freedom Trail is a walking tour of 16 historic buildings, sites and monuments that document Boston's contribution to American history. It is marked with a red line in the form of red bricks and red footsteps. The map shows most of them.

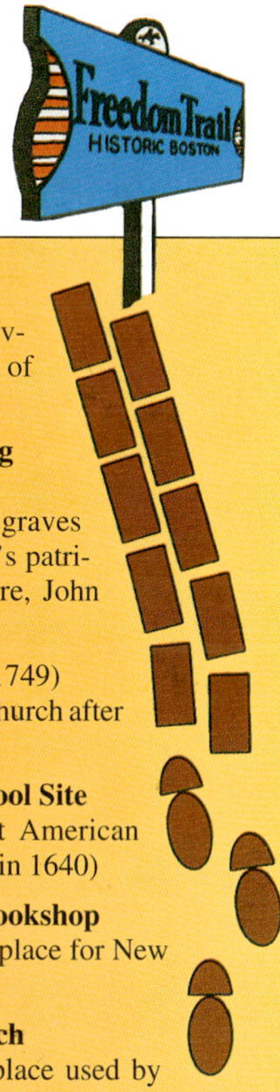

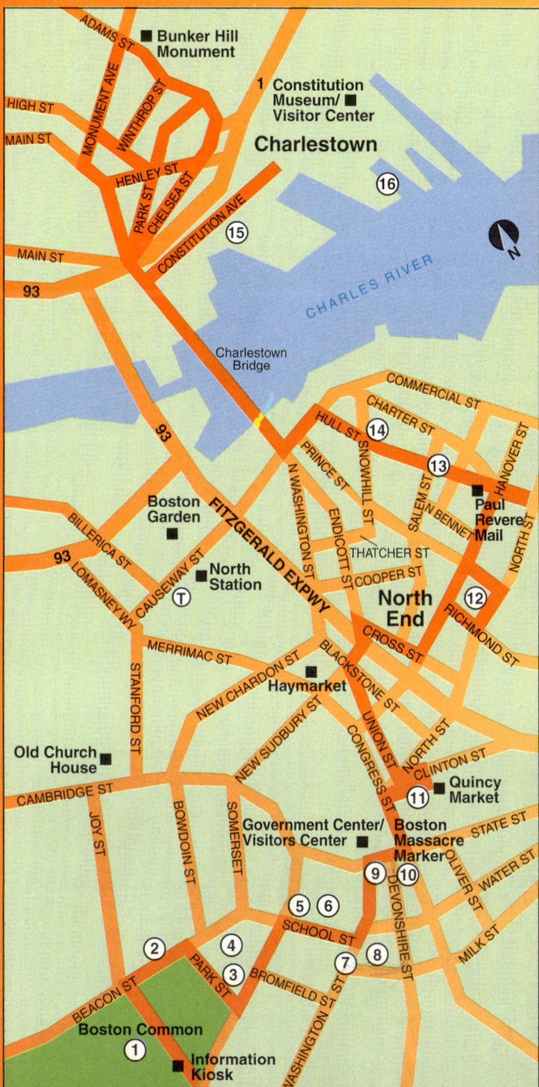

② **State House**
The seat of the Government of the State of Massachusetts

④ **Granary Burying Ground**
A churchyard with graves of some of America's patriots, e. g. Paul Revere, John Hancock and others

⑤ **King's Chapel** (1749)
The First Unitarian church after the Revolution

⑥ **First Public School Site**
The site of the first American Public School (built in 1640)

⑦ **Globe Corner Bookshop**
(1712) The meeting place for New England authors

⑧ **Old South Church**
(1670). A meeting place used by colonists

⑨ **Old State House**
(1713) The seat of the Colonial Government

⑩ **Boston Massacre Site**
The site where colonists were killed by British soldiers

⑪ **Faneuil Hall** (1742)
A meeting place, also called the Cradle of Liberty

⑫ **Paul Revere House**
(1676) Oldest house in Boston, Paul Revere's home

⑬ **Old North Church** (1723)
The city's oldest church in use

⑮ **Bunker Hill Monument**
An obelisk in commemoration of the first major battle of the Revolution

In the light of what you know about Boston and its history, try to explain why these sights are part of the Freedom Trail.

Project An illustrated leaflet

Make a leaflet showing the different sides of Boston. You may think about its various aspects, old and new, its tourist attractions and its history.
The collage should contain short texts of your own as well as illustrations. You can also write to:

- Massachusetts Tourist Information Center, 100 Cambridge Street Boston, MA 02202
- Greater Boston Convention and Tourist Bureau, Prudential Towers, Box 490, Boston, MA 02199
- Foreign Visitor Center, 15 State Street, Boston MA 02116

and ask for further information. (letter-writing: for help see pp. 76ff.)

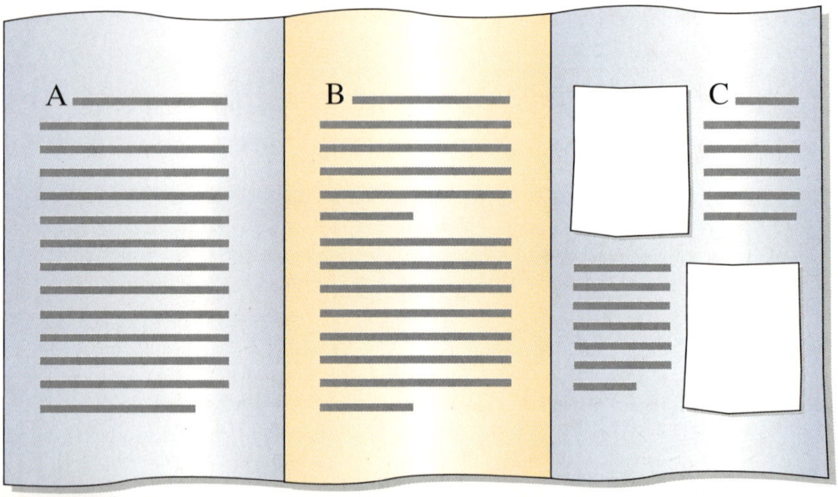

Unit 5 Why do people say what they say the way they say it?

Getting into the Unit

Do you use the same language
- when you talk to your brother or to your teacher?
- when you write a letter to your friend or to the editor of a newspaper?
- when you talk about a car accident or write a report on it?

People use different varieties[1] of language in different situations. These varieties are called *registers*[2]. Non-native speakers often use language from the wrong register or mix up language from different registers.
When we make contact with people we have to choose a register. We can either speak or write to them. When writing we usually have time to think about what and how we write, while in speech we have no time to think.
The term[3] "register" is also used in connection with[4] formal and informal English. We choose a formal register when we use language for official or public purposes (e.g. speeches, business letters), while informal English is the language of private conversation or personal letters.

This is an **expository text.** An expository text explains something in detail.

A What types of register are mentioned in the text?

[1]**variety** different kinds of language – [2]**register** different levels of language – [3]**term** a word or expression – [4]**in connection with** when we talk about

Registers
The varieties of language people use in different situations are called registers.

Registers

1. A conversation and a letter

Note down all the words or expressions which you think are typical of spoken or written English.

A conversation

Mrs B: They're going to have to do something about the traffic in Brampton. It was so crowded this morning, wasn't it – couldn't get across the road.

Mr B: I know. I got stuck in a traffic-jam on the way home. It took half an hour to get round the roundabout today.

Mrs B: Well, I think they ought to ban cars from the town centre, and give us a decent bus service.

Mr B: Hold on! It's all right for you, but how would I get to work? My office is on the other side of town. And what would happen if I had to work at night?

Mrs B: Hm … I don't know. The government ought to come up with a few ideas. Anyway. That's what we pay them for. All I know is that it's so crowded you can't move. You could cycle to work.

Mr B: What? In this weather?

A letter

There is an urgent need to limit the use of cars in cities without hindering mobility and causing economic disruption. Alternative forms of transport must be found, particularly for the motorised commuter travelling alone in a separate vehicle. Local and national governments are considering various plans to reduce urban congestion, including the provision of more efficient bus services.

2. Two letters

Note down the words or expressions which you think are formal or informal English in these two letters.

Dear Sir,

It was with deep regret that we learnt of the death of the Chairman of your Company last week. We have enjoyed a professional relationship with your firm for over a quarter of a century, and we greatly appreciate what his loss must mean to you all.
Please convey our condolences to his wife and family, and to the Board of Directors.

Yours faithfully,
G. R. White

Dear Peter,

I was ever so sorry to hear that your grandfather died last week. I know you were very fond of him. I only met him once but he seemed a very kind and friendly person. I'm sure you will miss him very much. Please give my regards to your parents and tell them that I'm thinking of you all. Write to me as soon as you can.

Yours affectionately,
Margaret

Summary

formal/informal English – spoken/written English

The following lists show some of the differences between these types of language.

spoken English	written English
informal words	formal words
incomplete sentences (e.g. Lovely to see you.)	complex sentences (e.g. It would be delightful to see you again if you could visit us soon.)
short forms (e.g. isn't, can't, didn't)	no short forms (e.g. is not, cannot, did not)
fillers (e.g. er …, um …, hm …, well …)	no fillers
tags (e.g. … isn't she?)	no tags

informal English	formal English
simple and informal words (e.g. <u>blooming</u> nonsense)	formal words (e.g. <u>absolute</u> nonsense)
short sentences (e.g. I came home at six. Then I read the paper.)	complex sentences (e.g. Having come home I read the paper.)
personal style (e.g. first and second person reference: I, you; questions. Can you come to our meeting at two o'clock?)	impersonal style (e.g. The meeting was fixed for two p.m.)

Can you solve the problem?

Here are some examples of the two registers. Tick the two correct boxes:

Dear Sir or Madam, would you please be so kind as to send me some information about Brighton where I intend to spend my holiday.	❑ spoken ❑ written ❑ informal ❑ formal
Dear John, it's been ages[1] since we've seen you. Why don't you come over next weekend?	❑ spoken ❑ written ❑ informal ❑ formal
Sorry, can't tell you the way to the station.	❑ spoken ❑ written ❑ informal ❑ formal
I am honoured to welcome you to this meeting. I'd like to express my thanks to all of you for joining us today.	❑ spoken ❑ written ❑ informal ❑ formal
It was not in fact John that did it.	❑ spoken ❑ written ❑ informal ❑ formal
Morgan to Stephens: a brilliant pass, that. Er ... And the score still: Bournemouth 4, Brentford 1.	❑ spoken ❑ written ❑ informal ❑ formal
Our distinguished[2] guests are requested[3] to ascend[4] to the second floor.	❑ spoken ❑ written ❑ informal ❑ formal
Up you get, you fellows.	❑ spoken ❑ written ❑ informal ❑ formal

[1]**it's been ages** it's long ago – [2]**distinguished** important, famous – [3]**to request** to ask sb. to do sth. – [4]**to ascend** to go up

Writer's Workshop

This workshop will help you to write different kinds of English texts.

Note-taking

Note-taking (i.e. writing sth. down) is not only a common exercise which is done at school to help you to understand a text that you have read or heard, but also a useful technique in real life.
There are three types of note-taking:
You can write down
- as many details as possible, or
- the main points, or
- special aspects of a text.

Here is an example

The text *(The Big Race, pp. 10f., ll. 4–14)*

As I walked into the changing rooms, taking a basket for my clothes on the way, I noticed a man and a boy sitting in one corner, talking. I recognised the boy – he was called Gordon Hayes and I had swum against him before. He was fast – his best time for two lengths' backstroke was only one second slower than mine. He was tall with long legs and strong muscles. He had a pleasant face which was topped by a shock of dark brown hair. The man, who I assumed was his father, was the opposite. He was short and stocky with an almost square face and a rapidly receding hairline. I stood still, just out of their line of vision.

Note-taking

a) Writing down as many details as possible

- narrator sees man and boy when walking to changing room
- both talking
- boy's name: Gordon Hayes
- fast swimmer, one second slower than narrator
- tall and strong
- pleasant face, dark brown hair

etc.

b) Writing down the main points

- (narrator) sees man and boy
- they talk to each other
- boy: pleasant; man: unpleasant

etc.

c) Writing down special points

Gordon Hayes	*father*
tall	short
strong	stocky
fast swimmer	square face
pleasant face	receding hair line
dark brown hair	

What to do

Before writing
Step 1 Read the text and try to understand what it is all about.
Step 2 Read the text again, this time very slowly, and find the main points.

While writing
- When you come across examples or facts, take notes under appropriate headings (all details, main points or special points).
- Put down keywords only and not complete sentences.

After writing
Check your notes by comparing them with the text.

Writing a paragraph

A **paragraph** is a group of sentences dealing with one topic[1] only. In a good paragraph ideas are developed logically and put into sentences that are connected[2] by connectives[3] (e. g. while, in other words, furthermore, etc.) so that the reader will be able to follow the presentation of the writer's ideas step by step.

Here is an example

Leisure

It is rather interesting to see how people spend their free time.
Most people in this town spend a great deal of their leisure time at home **but** they are also very regular cinema and concert goers. A lot of young people belong to clubs and some to study circles, **too**. Sports and outdoor recreations are popular: walking, swimming, skiing **as well as** home-centred activities such as gardening.
As shown above there are lots of different ways of spending your free time in an interesting way.

< one topic only

< topic sentence at the beginning

< ideas in a logical order, ideas and sentences linked up by connectives

< concluding sentence

[1]**topic** sth. to talk or write about – [2]**to connect** to bring together – [3]**connective** a word or phrase that connects words or sentences

This is a list of sentence connectives:

When you want to ...	use:
add ideas	moreover, furthermore, and, similarly, in addition to this, ...
give reasons	therefore, so, that is why, ...
refer to sth.	referring to, as to, as for, with regard to, according to, ...
want to say sth. in order words	that means, in other words, that is to say, ...
show order	first, firstly, secondly, next, finally, ...
show consequence	it follows that, thus, consequently, as a result, therefore, ...
say sth. against a statement	on the other hand, but, however, in spite of the fact, on the contrary, ...

Summary-writing

A **summary** is the short version of a text which only contains the most important information.

Here is an example

The complaint

The restaurant-car staff on long-distance trains seem to belong to an arrogant race. They tend to look down on their passengers. Only a brave and courageous man will argue with a dining-car waiter and complain to a foreigner in his native tongue. But an act of heroism was performed by a Spaniard who dared to question the tenderness of a steak served to him in the dining-car of the Madrid-Paris express. The French head-waiter appeared and said he could not understand the complaint. The Spaniard insisted, however, and finally the waiter informed him that there was a "suggestions and complaints box" at the end of the car. The Spaniard thanked him politely and then, seizing the steak from his plate, walked down the car and stuffed it into the complaints box.

Outline	Summary
Restaurant-car waiters' attitudes towards passengers	Restaurant-car waiters behave arrogantly, to whom only the bravest passengers dare to complain.
A Spaniard's complaint	But one day a Spaniard, on the Madrid-Paris express, does complain. He is not happy with his steak.
The head-waiter's reaction	The head-waiter says he cannot understand him but tells him that there is a complaints box at the end of the car.
The complaints box	On hearing this the Spaniard takes the steak and pushes it into the box.

What to do

Before writing

Step 1 Read the original text carefully in order to understand it in every detail.

Step 2 Find the main ideas in the text and underline them. Mark the parts of the text that can be left out, for example:
– statistics, facts, dates, examples, anecdotes, quotations[1], detailed descriptions, stylistic means such as repetition, exaggeration, irony, examples of figurative language, etc.

Step 3 Make a topic outline.

While writing

- Write the summary from the author's point of view.
- Make sure that you produce a text that follows the order of the original, but try to use your own words as much as possible. Your summary should not be just a list of notes but connected sentences (for help see p. 69).
- When necessary, change direct speech into reported speech.
- Use the present tense.
- Do not add new material such as your own opinion or interpretation.

After writing

Checklist:

- Have you only included the most important ideas of the original text?
- Have you left out your own impressions or opinions?
- Have you connected the sentences well?
- Will your summary be clear to somebody who does not know the original text?

[1]**quotation** the word-by-word reproduction of sentences from the original text or of what people have said

Characterization

People's (or – in fictional texts – the characters') social position, their situation as well as their outward appearance, behaviour, words and thoughts, feelings and attitudes are all aspects of a **characterization:** They are all connected with each other in order to give a full and complex idea of the character. The reactions of other people (or other characters in the text) also add to the characterization.

immer in present – direkte Rede kann stehen, weil sie charakterisieren kann

Here is an example

The text is an excerpt taken from *The Big Race* (cf. pp. 10f.). Read it carefully and pay special attention to the words that are underlined. This will help you to understand the characterization on p. 72.

As I walked into the changing rooms, taking a basket for my clothes on the way, I noticed a man and a boy sitting in one corner, talking. I recognised the boy – he was called Gordon Hayes and I had swum against him before. He was fast – his best time for two lengths' backstroke was only one second slower than mine. He was tall with long legs and strong muscles. He had a pleasant face which was topped by a shock of dark brown hair. The man, who I assumed was his father, was the opposite. He was short and stocky with an almost square face and a rapidly receding hairline. I stood still, just out of their line of vision. Something told me I should not disturb them. I heard the end of the conversation, although I had no real desire to spy on them.

Gordon's father said: 'If you divven't win that race I'll really belt yer one!'

'But, Dad ...'

'No buts. You can beat that lad from Durham.'

'But I can't.'

'You will or else.'

Then his father stomped off, leaving Gordon curled up in the corner, shaking like a leaf. I walked up to him and said innocently: 'What's the matter?'

'It's him. He says he'll hit me if I don't beat you in the backstroke.'

'I'm sure he wouldn't. You are his son.'

'He will.'

'Well, if you just do your best that's all anyone can ask for.'

'My best won't be good enough,' he said hopelessly.

1. Notes

outward appearance	behaviour	words and thoughts	feelings and attitudes	others' reactions
tall, long legs, strong muscles, a pleasant face, dark brown hair	talks with his father, curled up in a corner, shakes "like a leaf"	does not think that he will win	insecure, very unhappy, miserable, afraid of his father, hopeless	the narrator's respect for Gordon's best time, his father's threats, the narrator's pity

2. Characterization

Gordon Hayes is one of several boys taking part in a swimming race (cf. ll. 1ff.).
He is tall and strong (cf. l. 4) and a very good swimmer: "He was fast – his best time for two lengths' backstroke was only one second slower than mine (i. e. the narrator's)." (ll. 3f.)
But he does not think that he will be able to win this race because he knows that the narrator can swim faster than he can: "My best won't be good enough." (l. 20)
The talk with his father before the race makes Gordon feel insecure and very unhappy because his father threatens to beat him if he does not win (cf. ll. 9ff.).
Gordon is afraid of his father: His father's threats make him shake "like a leaf" (l.14). This comparison marks a significant contrast between Gordon's outward appearance and his feelings. The fact that he curls up in a corner after his father has left him (cf. ll. 14f.) shows that he is scared of his father's violence. He knows that his father will carry out his threat because he seems to have done so before (cf. l. 18). So Gordon feels hopeless and miserable (cf. l. 20).
The narrator feels pity for Gordon, perhaps because of the fact that Gordon seems to be a nice boy – he has a "pleasant face" (ll. 4f.). He tries to cheer him up: "... if you just do your best that's all anyone can ask for." (ll. 19f.), but he is not able to make him forget his father's threats.
At this stage of the story it seems to be impossible for Gordon to avoid his father's punishment although he is an excellent swimmer.

Introduction
(The character's situation)
Development
(outward appearance and abilities)
(words and thoughts)
(feelings and attitudes)
(others' reactions)
Concluding sentence
(summary of results)

What to do

Before writing

Step 1 Read the text carefully. Mark the words or sentences or write down the lines that give you information about the character(s).

Step 2 Draw a chart that includes columns like "situation/position", "outward appearance", "behaviour", "words/thoughts", "feelings/attitudes", "others' reactions" or – if you compare characters – "similarities" and "differences" (cf. p. 35) and fill in your notes.

Step 3 Ask yourself if the character(s) change(s) during the development of the text and if so, how.

Step 4 Number your notes and group them.

While writing

Step 1 Write a short introduction in which you present the character(s) and his or her (their) situation.

Step 2 Organize your notes into paragraphs. Every paragraph should deal with one characteristic feature[1]. Present the evidence[2] taken from the text and comment on it. Don't forget to refer to or quote the text.

Step 3 Try to show how the different characteristic features belong together.

Step 4 Write a conclusion that sums up the results of your detailed analysis.

After writing

Checklist:

- Does your introduction lead to the detailed analysis of one or more characters?
- Does your characterization include all the notes that you made before starting to write?
- Have you linked up the different aspects in a logical way?
- Have you referred to or quoted the text?
- Does your conclusion offer a convincing summary of what you have found?

Giving opinions

We can either write or talk about our **opinions**[3] on a topic. We have to distinguish[4] between short, mostly spoken comments and written, longer forms of expressing our opinions. The written form usually has the following parts: a) presenting the topic, b) giving opinions, c) supporting[5] opinions by facts, examples, etc., d) conclusion.

Here is an example

Walking by oneself in Boston — topic

People say that the City of Boston is very safe. The police are on patrol downtown and in the neighborhoods day and night.

But I think there is nevertheless some risk when you walk around by yourself at night. — personal opinion

It is especially the side-streets and The Boston Common, Boston's big park, that are not safe enough. I believe — facts to support opinion

....

....

....

Therefore, I would not dare to walk through the streets at night, not even with friends. — conclusion

[1]**characteristic feature** (e.g. friendliness, carelessness, imagination, etc. are all characteristic features) – [2]**evidence** words or sentences taken from the text that show that your interpretation is right – [3]**opinion** what you believe or think about sth. – [4]**to distinguish** to see a difference between two things – [5]**to support** here: *begründen*

What to do

Before writing

Step 1 Write down your opinion of the problem.
Step 2 Find facts, examples, etc. to support your opinion.
If you have to give your opinion on a problem that is dealt with in a text you may find some ideas in the text itself.
Step 3 Put the points which you found in a logical order.
Step 4 Think about the opposite position and try to find arguments to reject[1] it.
Step 5 Find a good conclusion.

While writing

Step 1 Begin your statement with an introduction to the problem.
(The problem/topic I am going to deal with is ..., I am going to deal with ...)
Step 2 Give your own opinion.
(In my opinion ..., To my mind ..., I think ...)
Step 3 Support your opinion by the facts you have found.
(The first point to mention is ..., I would like to give examples ..., With regard to..., Furthermore, ..., On the other hand ..., In connection with ..., I would like to refer to ...)
Step 4 Sum up the problem and your own opinion. (As a result ..., To sum up my arguments ...)

After writing

Checklist:
- Have you concentrated on your topic?
- Have you made your position clear enough?
- Are your arguments convincing?
- Can you add some more facts to support your opinion?
- Does your conclusion sum up your position without being just a repetition of what you have already said?

[1]**to reject** to say "no" to sth.

Story-telling

A **story** consists of three main parts: the introduction, the development of the action and the ending.

Here is an example

Locker 160

Karen and Julie have the idea of playing a nasty trick on Miriam, one of their classmates, by putting a hate note in her locker.

They keep on doing unkind things to her during the next few days.

Miriam reacts by attempting to commit suicide.

This is the pattern:

- *Introduction* (exposition): presenting the characters, the setting and the situation
- *Development* (rising action, climax): showing a growing conflict or problem through action
- *Ending* (turning point, falling action, dénouement): solving the conflict

What to do

Before writing

Step 1 Collect ideas on characters, setting, conflict, etc.
Step 2 Make notes for the three main parts (introduction, development, ending).
Step 3 Find a title for your story.

While writing

- Choose a narrator and tell the story from his/her point of view (cf. p. 25).
- Use the past tense.
- Use connectives (see p. 69).
- Use adjectives or adverbs to make your story vivid[1].
- Try to use direct speech.

After writing

Checklist:

- Does your title fit[2] the story?
- Are your descriptions vivid enough?
- Does the action develop in a logical way?
- Did you divide your story into paragraphs?
- Did you connect paragraphs and sentences?

[1]**vivid** lively – [2]**to fit** to go well with

Letter-writing

Letters may be divided into two main types: personal letters (e.g. to a friend) and formal letters (e.g. to the editor of a newspaper, business letters). A letter usually consists[1] of four parts: a) address and date, b) salutation, c) body of letter, d) ending and name.

Here is an example

A personal letter

24, Lynford Avenue Winchester, Hants, SO226BN	address
October 26th, ...	date
Dear John,	salutation[a]
Now that I've been home for a few days, I thought I had better write and let you know again how sorry I am about my behaviour at your party last week.	reasons for writing
I danced with Mary a lot – and we had a nice chat. I didn't know that she was your girlfriend and that you would be hurt. But when you told me I immediately said that I had to talk to another friend. I've already written to Mary and explained everything to her. Please don't be angry. I promise that this will not happen again.	body of letter[b]
I hope that you will accept this explanation[2] of what happened and that you will write back to tell me so.	closing remarks[c]
Yours,	ending
David	name

[1]**to consist of** to be made up of, to have – [2]**explanation** saying why sth. was done

[a]**salutation** greeting by words – [b]**body of letter** the main part of a letter – [c]**closing remarks** a sentence or sentences at the end of the main part of the letter

What to do

Before writing
Step 1 Collect ideas for your letter.
Step 2 Put your ideas in a good order.

While writing
- Choose the appropriate speech level (cf. pp. 64f.).
- Connect your ideas by connectives.

After writing
Checklist:
- Have you put your ideas in a logical order (see step 2)?
- Have you connected your sentences?
- Have you used the layout given above?

Diary-writing

A **diary** is a collection of personal experiences and comments on events, people, feelings, etc. It is usually written every day. Sometimes the form of a diary is used to present a fictional story.

Here is an example

This is the beginning of Rob's diary entry for the day of his bicycle ride with his father (cf. *Manhood*, pp. 15ff.)

Sunday

What a day!
What happened today has really made me so unhappy ... And it all started so nicely. Dad asked me to go on a bike ride this morning and I said ok because the weather was fine and I thought it might be a nice idea. If I had only known what he was up to I should have guessed that this bike ride would not be a pleasant one because Dad always tries to make me do some training and I'm not so sure if I really share his enthusiasm ...

- day
- beginning
- an experience (first person singular)
- personal remarks

What to do

Before writing
Step 1 Choose the date and the event(s) that you want to write about. Put them in a logical order.
Step 2 Make notes on your personal reactions, thoughts, feelings, point of view, opinion, etc.

While writing
- Use an interesting beginning.
- Use the first person singular.
- Use the past tense.
- Make sure that you write the whole entry from your own point of view.
- Include vivid details, exclamations and/or questions that show it.
  If you write a diary entry for a fictional character try to put yourself in his or her shoes.
- Collect from the text all the information that shows the character's experiences, opinions, feelings, etc.
- Decide which ideas should be included in the diary.
- Perhaps add more ideas that illustrate[1] the character's attitude.

After writing
Checklist:
- Does the entry deal with[2] all the important events?
- Have you included words and expressions which give the diary entry a private character?
- Does your diary entry match the thoughts, comments, feelings, etc. of the character?

Writing a newspaper article

A **newspaper article** (esp. a report) informs the reader about what happened somewhere. It gives answers to the five "W's" and an "H" *("Who did what, when, where, why and how?")*. Reports have to be objective but there are also articles that only want to entertain[3] the reader.

Here is an example

Teenager attacked on way home from disco

A 16-year-old girl was attacked and robbed on her way home from a disco last night. She was taken to hospital, but released[4] soon afterwards with minor injuries[5].

Jane Jackson spent the evening at a local disco not far from her home. She left before her friends because she had promised not to be home late. As she was walking through a park she was attacked by a man she later described as dark-haired and in his early thirties. The man took her money and her watch. Luckily, a car was just passing by when the attack happened. The driver stopped and went to help the girl while the thief ran off.

The police have often warned teenagers not to walk through the park alone after dark. "Jane Jackson had a narrow escape[6], but it might be worse next time", a police officer told our reporter.

- *headline*
- *introduction:* a short summary of the story answering the *who*, *what*, *where* and *when* questions
- *the story in detail:* the *why* and *how* questions
- *ending:* summary, comment or quotation from sb.

[1]**to illustrate** to show – [2]**to deal with** to be about – [3]**to entertain** to amuse – [4]**to release** to allow to go – [5]**injury** *Verletzung* – [6]**to have a narrow escape** to avoid a danger that nearly happened

What do do

Before writing

Step 1 Choose the topic you are going to write about.

Step 2 Decide whether you are going to write an article to inform or to entertain the reader and think about how you can make it objective or entertaining and sensational.

Step 3 Make notes about the "who", "what", "where", "when" and, if possible, the "why" and "how" of the event.

Step 4 Decide on the order of the different points.

While writing

- Begin your article with an introduction to the event.
- Use your notes while writing the article.
- Divide your article into paragraphs.
- Include adjectives, adverbs, etc. and, if possible, say what other people said about the event.
- Find a short conclusion, but do not use the first person singular – make it neutral.
- Find an attractive headline.

After writing

Checklist:

- Does your article contain enough detailed information or can you add some more?
- Is the article easy to understand and interesting?
- Is the headline attractive?
- Have you connected your ideas and sentences (see p. 69)?

Comparing texts

When two texts are to be compared similarities and differences should be taken into consideration. This means that the topic, the meaning, the intention and the effect of the texts have to be considered as well as their structure, the choice of words and the respective use of stylistic devices.

What to do

Before writing

Step 1 Read the two texts carefully again. While reading make notes on differences and/or similarities as far as topic, meaning and the authors' intentions are concerned.

Step 2 Using different colours mark those lines which show similarities and/or differences in the choice of words and/or stylistic devices or draw a chart in order to take notes.

Step 3 Read all your notes again to see what can be grouped together in order to show the relationship between the meaning of the two texts and their form.

Step 4 Number your notes and group them.

Step 5 Organize your notes into paragraphs. Every paragraph should deal with one specific aspect of your comparison only.

While writing

Step 1 Write a short introduction in which you briefly state what the two texts have in common as far as their topic is concerned. You can start like this:
Both texts are about ...
Both texts refer to ...
There are similarities between the texts along the following lines ...

Step 2 On the basis of your interpretation of one text give a detailed analysis of the second one by pointing out similarities and differences. These expressions may help you:
(The second text) also tells us about/describes/evokes .../begins/ends with ...
(Un)like *(author's name),* (author's name) uses ... in order to.../ wants the reader to.../expresses his/her opinion about...
(*The second text*), (un)like (the first one), appeals to the reader to...
Whereas (author's name) speaks about/refers to..., (*author's name*) describes/deals with/talks about...
In contrast to (author's name), *(author's name) ...*

Step 3 Try to show that the meaning of the texts and the way they are written depend on each other.

Step 4 Write a conclusion that sums up the results of your detailed comparison.

After writing

Checklist:
- Does your introduction lead to a detailed comparison of the two texts?
- Does your comparison include all the notes that you made before starting to write?
- Have you linked up the different aspects in a logical way?
- Have you referred to or quoted the text(s)?
- Does your conclusion offer a convincing summary of what you have found?

Glossary of Terms for Text Analysis

act	the major unit in the action of a full-length play. Acts in a play are comparable to chapters in a book.
acting time	the time the action of a narrative lasts (cf. reading time)
action	action in fictional texts is everything that happens in a story, drama, etc. It may be external, when the writer describes what the characters do and/or say, or it may be internal, when the writer shows the thoughts and feelings of the characters.
antithesis	the presentation of a contrasting idea or argument
alliteration	the repetition of an initial sound in a sequence of words, e.g. ... is **r**unning **r**ound ...
allusion	a reference to a well-known work of literature, a famous person, or a historical event which the reader is supposed to know
assonance	the repetition of vowel sounds within two or more words, e.g. I l**ie** down b**y** the s**i**de ...
atmosphere	the feeling or mood created by the author through the description of events, setting, situation, etc.
blank verse	unrhymed poetry written with an alternating pattern of stressed and unstressed syllables. The rhythm created by this pattern resembles the natural rhythm of spoken English.
catastrophe	the unfortunate or disastrous end of a story or play
character	a person who takes part in the action of a fictional text – flat character: a character in a literary work who does not develop in the course of the action; round character: complex individual who may change
characterization	the author may present his characters in two ways: – directly by describing them, or – indirectly through their actions, thoughts or feelings and words.
climax/crisis	the moment at which the action comes to its point of greatest intensity, the moment that determines whether the situation will improve or grow worse (cf. turning-point). Crisis refers to the highest point of reader interest.
comedy	a type of play which deals with a light or serious topic in an amusing way, always with a happy ending
comic relief	a humorous scene, incident, or speech in the course of a serious literary work that relieves the tension momentarily
conflict	the struggle between opposing forces which is the basis of the plot of a story or play. External conflict occurs between two characters, or between a character and society. Internal conflict occurs when a character struggles within himself or herself, in order to make a decision.
content	the kind of information a text contains
dialect	the form of language as it is spoken in a certain place or among a certain group of people
dialogue	a conversation between two or more characters
drama	see ‚play‘

ellipsis	the omission of essential grammatical elements (e.g. So early come?)
exaggeration	an extreme overstatement
exposition	the first part in a story or play that provides background information and introduces the story's setting, its conflict and often its main character or characters
falling action	the part of a story or play following the crisis/climax and leading to the dénouement or catastrophe
fiction	a piece of writing that comes from a writer's imagination. Fiction is not factual but may be sometimes based on facts, real experiences or people the writer has known.
figurative language	language that conveys meaning beyond the literal meaning of the words. Writers often use figurative language to create effects, to emphasize ideas and to call upon emotions (see simile, metaphor and personification).
free verse	poetry without regular patterns of rhyme and metre. It often sounds like everyday language when it is read aloud.
function of a text	intention of a text; possible functions are to amuse, to criticise, to inform, to persuade, etc.
genre	the term used to specify the distinct types or categories into which literary works are grouped. The four main literary genres are fiction, poetry, drama and non-fiction.
humour	in literature: an amusing description, an exaggeration, or a sarcastic remark
image	a picture in words. Images (symbol, simile and metaphor) are examples of figurative language. The words that are used mean more than their usual definition in a dictionary.
introduction	the beginning of any text (cf. exposition)
irony	the contrast between what is said and what is really meant
metaphor	an implicit comparison between two things or ideas, not introduced by 'as' or 'like' (e.g. the river of life)
metre	the regular pattern of stressed and unstressed syllables in a line of poetry, e.g. – iambic metre: short syllable followed by a long one – anapaestic feet: short syllables followed by a long one – trochaic feet: long syllable followed by a short one – free verse: no fixed metre
mood	the feeling that the writer tries to evoke in a work of literature, such as excitement, anger, sadness, happiness, pity, etc.
motive	a character's reason for action
narrative	any writing that tells a story
narrator	a fictitious person who tells the story
non-fiction	prose writing about real people, places, things and ideas
open ending	a structural element in fictional texts in which the conflict remains for the most part unresolved
paragraph	a group of several interrelated sentences in a non-fictional text
personification	type of figurative language in which human qualities are attributed to an object, animal or idea

play	a piece of literature that is written to be presented on a stage. In a drama or play actors and actresses play the roles of the characters, telling the story through their words and actions. Like fiction, a play contains character(s), setting, plot and theme. A full-length play is divided into acts and scenes.
plot	the sequence of actions and events in a literary work. The emphasis lies on causality (cause – effect), e.g.: The king died, and then the queen died of *grief*. Compare 'story': a sequence of events in which the emphasis is on *time*, e.g.: The king died, and then the queen died.
poetry	special type of literature in which words are chosen and arranged in single lines to create a certain effect. Poems often reflect the speaker's experiences or like fiction, they can also tell stories.
point of view	the perspective from which a story is presented. The story can be told by a first-person or by a third-person narrator. The narrator can be a character in or outside the story.
protagonist	the main character in a fictional text
reading time	the time it takes a person to read a story or play
register	level of language
rhyme	the repetition of sounds at the end of two or more lines or in the middle of a poem's lines: – full rhyme: show – blow – eye rhyme: dies – stories (only the spelling suggests a rhyming pattern)
rhyme scheme	the pattern created by rhymes rhyming couplets: recall (a) all (a) night (b) light (b) sky (a) show (b) blow (b) alternate rhyme: crow (a) me (b) snow (a) tree (b) embracing rhyme: tree (a) another (b) weather (b) me (a)
rhythm	the regular or irregular stress pattern in a line of a poem
rising action	the part of a play or story following the exposition and leading to the climax
scene	part of an act in a play
setting	the place where and time at which the action takes place, and the social background of the characters
short play	a (one-act) play concentrating on a single dramatic situation, one place, a short time-span, a small cast of characters and one main conflict. Normally a short play is not divided into smaller parts like a full-length play.

short story	a work of fiction which usually deals with one or two major characters and one major conflict. The elements of a short story are character, plot, setting and theme. In short stories there is often a surprise ending.
simile	a comparison between different things or ideas indicated by 'like' or 'as' e.g. Her lips are as red as roses.
slang	very informal, often vulgar but lively level of speech outside the standard version of a language
structure	the organization of the elements of a text
stage directions	notes in a play telling the actors how to speak and act. They also say what the characters and the stage should look like and where and when the action takes place.
stanza	a group of lines that form a unit in a poem, often called a verse
style	the special, often personal and individual way in which a writer expresses ideas, often in close connection with the type of text he/she has chosen
suspense	growing feeling of excitement that makes a reader curious about the outcome of a story
symbol	an object, a character or an event that stands for an abstract idea or suggests something greater than itself, e. g. the cross as the symbol of Christianity
tension	the feeling caused by the conflict of opposing forces in a text
text form	the classification of a text according to the form in which it is presented, e.g. as a poem, a short story, a play, a report, etc.
text type	the classification of the text according to the writer's intentions. There are five different models of text types: description (presenting the characteristics of living things, objects or processes), narration (presenting actions or events in a logical temporal order), exposition (explaining relatively complex matter in an objective and precise way), argumentation (dealing with problems and expressing reasons for a particular opinion), instruction (telling sb. what to do).
theme	the main generalized idea the writer wants to present. As the theme is usually not stated directly, the reader has to figure it out. One way of discovering the theme of a story is to consider what happens to the main character(s) and what it all means to him/her/them.
topic sentence	the sentence that expresses the main idea of the paragraph in which it occurs
turning point	the point at which the action takes a different, often unexpected direction

Vocabulary for Text Analysis and Text Production

Appendix 3

The following words and phrases will help you to talk about texts, to interpret short stories, plays and poems, to analyse non-fictional texts and to do written tasks.

Fictional Texts: short story, play, poem

theme

The story / play / poem deals with ...

The theme of the story / play / poem is ...

action and plot

The setting of the story / play is ...

The action of the story / play is set in ...

The action takes place in ...

The events of the story happen ...

The main elements of the plot are ...

The stages / phases of the action are ...

The turning point / climax is reached when ...

The action reaches its climax when ...

The story has a surprise / tragic / happy ending.

atmosphere

The atmosphere of the play / story is ..., because ...

The setting / description of ... creates a/an ... atmosphere.

calm	(ruhig)	aggressive	(aggressiv)
carefree	(sorgenfrei)	cold	(kalt)
peaceful	(friedlich)	dark	(dunkel)
safe	(sicher)	gloomy	(schwermütig)
serene	(heiter)	tense	(gespannt)
		threatening	(drohend)
		sad	(traurig)

The	author narrator	describes the	characteristic features activities outward appearance	of ...	✓ characterization

The following characteristics are typical	aspects features	of ...

The main character's behaviour is	polite. ...

✓ character: trait (positive/negative)

(positive)		(negative)	
balanced	(ausgeglichen)	aggressive	(aggressiv)
calm	(ruhig)	brutal	(brutal)
courageous	(mutig)	cruel	(grausam)
friendly	(freundlich)	desperate	(verzweifelt)
good-natured	(gutmütig)	impatient	(ungeduldig)
moderate	(gemäßigt)	impolite	(unhöflich)
modest	(bescheiden)	impulsive	(impulsiv)
patient	(geduldig)	intemperate	(unbeherrscht)
polite	(höflich)	intolerant	(intolerant)
reasonable	(vernünftig)	irritable	(reizbar)
self-controlled	(beherrscht)	obstinate	(eigensinnig)
self-assured	(selbstbewusst)	ruthless	(rücksichtslos)
sensible	(vernünftig)	self-centred	(ichbezogen)
sensitive	(empfindsam)	stubborn	(halsstarrig)
tolerant	(tolerant)	understanding	(verständnisvoll)
arrogant	(überheblich)		

✓ (feeling)

to be	concerned	(besorgt)	bothered	(verärgert)
	confident	(zuversichtlich)	excited	(aufgeregt)
	content	(zufrieden)	fearful	(furchtsam)
	hopeful	(hoffnungsvoll)	frightened	(erschrocken)
	optimistic	(optimistisch)	nervous	(nervös)
	patient	(geduldig)	pessimistic	(pessimistisch)
	pleased	(erfreut)	upset	(aufgeregt)
	satisfied	(zufrieden)	sad	(traurig)
	worried	(beunruhigt)	shocked	(schockiert)

Stylistic Features and Rhetorical Devices

The text is full of	abstract unusual colourful	words/expressions.	✓ choice of words

The author uses	images. poetic expressions.

The	figurative metaphorical	language creates an atmosphere of ...

The word ... is	effective to the point vague	because ...

The tone of the passage is	aggressive. alarming. colloquial. humorous. ironical. light. neutral. playful. serious. ...		tone
The author seems to have a	powerful vivid	imagination when he says ...	imagination
The author	employs uses	vivid images in order to ...	
A (e. g. he) is like B (e. g. his father)			simile/comparison
This simile is	drawn taken	from the world of ...	
The simile indicates that ...			
The author uses	metaphors metaphorical language	in order to ...	metaphor
The metaphor ... conveys[1] the meaning of ...			
A	symbolizes is a symbol of	B.	symbol
The writer uses repetition to drive his message home[2].			repetition
The repetition of the word ... emphasizes the fact that ...			
The author is repetitive when he says ...			
This text contains	unnecessary monotonous	repetitions.	
The author	employs uses	flashbacks in order to ...	flashback
This flashback helps the reader to understand that ...			
The character's past is	evoked[3] recalled	in a series of flashbacks.	

[1]**to convey** *übermitteln* – [2]**to drive a message home** *jemandem etwas nachdrücklich vermitteln* – [3]**to evoke** *hier: schildern*

Non-fictional Texts

The	topic	of the text is ...	topic
	main idea		

The text	deals with	...
	is about	

The	main	idea expressed in the text is ...
	general	
	...	

The text	is	divided into ... parts.	structure
	can be		

The text	consists of	... paragraphs.
	has	

The	paragraph	can be subdivided[1] into ... parts.
	passage	

The main	parts	of the text are ...
	elements	

The ... paragraph contains the	introduction.
	central problem.
	conclusion/solution.

A possible heading for this	section	is: ...
	paragraph	

The author	deals with	...	author and text
	discusses		(the content of the text)

The author gives an exact	analysis	of ...
	description	

The author wants to	show	the reader that ...	(the author's intention)
	convince		

The author gives his	personal opinion	on the	problem	of ...	(the author's opinion)
	idea		question		

The author	thinks	that ...
	believes	

The author's	opinion	is based on ...

The author	uses	the following argument(s):	(argumentation)

The author	rejects[2]	the following argument(s):

The author	comes to	the conclusion that ...
	draws	

[1]**to subdivide** *unterteilen* – [2]**to reject** *widerlegen*

Adjective – Adverb

Adjective

Mr White is a **careful** driver.
His car is very **safe.**

Adjectives modify nouns (**careful** driver) or are used after certain verbs, e.g. to be (is **safe**).

Adverb

Mr Smith **usually** drives fast.
His wife is **terribly** anxious about this.
But he drives more **carefully** than most drivers.
Only quite a few people drive **extremely** carelessly.

Adverbs modify a whole sentence (Mr Smith **usually** drives very fast), an adjective (**terribly** anxious), a verb (drives **carefully**) or an adverb (**extremely** carelessly).

Exercise 1: What people are like or how they behave

With the help of the elements of the chart below, make sentences using adjectives or adverbs, e.g. John treats animals badly. He is very rude.

is/was (a/an)	rude	
	bad	
	gentle	
	tidy	
treat animals	correct	student
drive	excellent	driver
walk to school	incredible	singer
do his/her/their homework	extreme	football hooligan
usually sing	careless	pianist
learn languages	(im)polite	customer
answer other people	bad	skater
answer the telephone	nasty	...
play football/billiards	soft	
recite poems	neat	
type	quick	
...	...	

Exercise 2: Mr Johnson, the managing director of a big firm

Fill in these words; change them, where necessary, into adverbs:
absolute, big, careful, efficient, expensive, extreme, fast, hard, important, impressive, lazy, often, slow, terrible, usual

Mr Johnson is the managing director of Johnson & Johnson Co. Ltd. He drives a ... Rover. It is a very ... car and looks ... . Mr Johnson works ... and he is never ... . While, for instance, he is having his car filled up, he ... makes some ... telephone calls. He thinks that he is one of the busiest men and that he works ... and does his job ... . He is ... in a ... hurry. He lives in a suburb, so he finds it ... necessary to have a ... car. He drives very ... but claims that he is an ... skilful driver and drives more ... than most ... drivers.

Present Perfect – Past Tense

Tom **has worked** in the garden today.	Yesterday he **worked** in the house.
today past --- (unfinished time) --- present	yesterday past ---(finished time) --- present
Present Perfect: action: connection with the present, or continuing into the present/future.	**Past Tense:** action: finished in the past

Present Perfect Continuous

Ann **has been playing** tennis since 2 o'clock. Peter **has been writing** letters for two hours.

We use the **Present Perfect Continuous** to say how long something has been happening.

for and since

Chris cannot play tennis because it has been raining **since** three o'clock.
for two hours.

since	**for**
since two o' clock since 1970 since Monday	for two hours for ten minutes for a long time
•	———→
since two o'clock (beginning of period)	**for** two hours (period)

Exercise 1: Past Tense or Present Perfect?

Form sentences, e.g. Jim has never played golf.

write to his/her friends play golf play tennis watch a horror film visit	never recently just ...	yesterday last week last month ...

Exercise 2: for or since?

Make up sentences, e.g. George has been out for a long time.

George has been out ... He has been waiting for his girlfriend ... for/since It has been raining ...	a long time three o'clock lunchtime ...

Exercise 3: An interview with a German living in England

Fill in the gaps.

You: When ... (come) to England?
Peter: I ... (be) here ... 1980. You see, I ... (live) in England ... a long time.
You: What ... (be) your first impressions?
Peter: Well, at first I ... (think) everything ... (be) quite different from Germany, but now ... (get) used to life in this country.
You: ... (live) all the time with English people?
Peter: No, the first two years ... (live) with a Scottish family. They ... (be) very helpful and they ... (teach) me English too.
I ... (get married) in 1982 and then ... (move) to Manchester. I ... (now live) in this city ... several years.

Exercise 4: Can you write your curriculum vitae?

Here are some keywords:
born on ... in ...; sisters, brothers; live in ... for/since ...; move to ...; start elementary school in...; grammar/comprehensive school; be at this school since/for ...; favourite subjects; learn English for/since...; study chemistry, physics, ... since/for...; future job; etc.

Present and Past Participles Replacing Relative Clauses

Do you know the boy	who is talking **talking**	to Mr Stuart?
The man	who was injured **injured**	in the accident is Mr Stuart.

Participles (present participles, e.g. talk**ing**, and past participles, e.g. injur**ed**) may replace relative clauses if both clauses have the same subject.

Exercise 1: Who are the people in the street?

Make up sentences from this table using participles, e.g. The man walking in the street is my uncle.

The	man	who is walking in the street	is...
	boy	who is driving down the street	
	girl	who has been stopped by a policeman	
	...	who has been given a lift	
		...	

Exercise 2: A tennis tournament

Complete these sentences using the following verbs:
sit – choose – play – represent – play – give – play – expect – play – devote
Put them in the correct form.

The boy ... at the end of the first row is Robert, one of the boys ... to represent Reading School at tennis. The tennis ... at this school is of a very high standard, so any boy ... the school has a good chance of success in the tournament ... each term. The tennis coaching ... at the school is first class. Most boys ... in the tournament are 17 but Robert is only 14. But he already has the strength ... from much older students. A boy ... as well as Robert cannot long remain unknown to people ... to tennis.

Exercise 3: A pop concert

Can you describe the people attending a pop concert? Use participles instead of relative clauses, e.g.: The people going to a pop concert are usually rather young.

Present and Past Participles Replacing Adverbial Clauses

After we had found our hotel		we looked for somewhere to have dinner.
Having found	our hotel	we looked for somewhere to have dinner.
After finding		

There was an interesting play at the theatre.
But because we had already seen the play twice, we did not go to the theatre.
Having seen the play twice we did not go to the theatre.

Because we felt tired we went to bed early.
Feeling tired we went to bed early.

Present and past participles can replace adverbial clauses. Note that these structures are mainly used in **written** English, **and will often sound very formal.**

Exercise 1: Make one sentence out of two

Begin like this: Having ...

We finished our work. Then we went home.
We had dinner. Then we left for the theatre.
We bought our tickets. Then we went into the theatre.
We saw a play. Then we had a drink at a pub.

This time begin with ... ing

He felt ill. So he took some pills.
He felt tired too. So he went to bed.
He had a terrible headache. He stayed in bed the next day.
He was well again after some days. So he went back to work.

Exercise 2: Henry Jackson's emigration

Can you rewrite these sentences in a more formal style?

Because Henry Jackson had lost his job in England, he emigrated to the United States. After he had moved to the States, he started working on a farm. But after some years he was sick of working on a farm, he moved to a nearby town. When he had thought everything over, he decided to work in a restaurant. He did this job for some time, then he moved to Boston. Because he was very intelligent, he decided to study medicine. He became a doctor.

Exercise 3: A story of your own

Write a short text describing the course of some events and try to replace some adverbial clauses by participles.

The Gerund

I'll do the shopping when I have finished **cleaning** the flat.
But before **leaving** I'll feed the dog.

Gerunds are formed by adding **-ing** to the infinitive.
Gerunds are used
– after certain verbs (e.g. hate writing, enjoy swimming)
– after prepositions (e.g. on hearing the news, fed up with studying)

Exercise 1: Make up sentences, using the gerund,
e.g.: He's fed up with learning foreign languages.

He's is not interested	about, at, in, of,	learning ...
He's not very good	with	going ...
He's fed up		studying ...
He's excited		doing ...
He did not think		helping ...
He's very fond		seeing ...
...	...	

Lots of people	don't	enjoy	watching ...
	never	finish	writing ...
	always	avoid	doing ...
	...	postpone	cleaning...
		...	having ...
			...

Exercise 2: An interview with a model

Fill in the gaps, using gerunds. These words may help you:
after return-, by tell-, enjoy meet-, fond of travel-, for be-, in model-, like get-, of do-, of los(e)-, of stand-, or be-, risk eat-, to work-

Miss Brandon: I must apologize ... ... late.
Reporter: That's all right. Perhaps you could start ... ... me how your career began.
Miss Brandon: I won a competition, though at that time I had no experience ... ...
Reporter: What do you enjoy about your job?
Miss Brandon: I'm very ... ... and I ... ... people. My job gives me the opportunity ... ... both.
Reporter: Do you never get tired ... ... in front of cameras?
Miss Brandon: No, I'm used ... ... long hours.
Reporter: Is there anything you don't like?
Miss Brandon: I don't ... ... up early. I can't ... ... everything I'd like to, because I have to watch my weight all the time.
Reporter: You travel a lot. Aren't you afraid ... ... your friends?
Miss Brandon: No, not really. ... ... home I go and see my friends.
Reporter: Thank you very much, Miss Brandon.

Exercise 3: About your holidays

Can you describe one of your most interesting or exciting holidays and say what you enjoyed, hated, avoided, didn't mind, etc. and what you were interested in, good at, fed up with, etc.? Use gerunds when possible.

Reported Speech

direct speech

Fred: "I **don't want** to have an operation because my headaches **have stopped**."

reported speech

Fred said that he **didn't want** an operation because his headaches **had stopped**.

When the introductory verb is in the Past Tense (e.g. said), there is a change in the tense of the reported speech.

direct speech	Present Tense (e.g. are)	Past Tense (e.g. was)	Present Perfect (e.g. has been)	Future (e.g. will be)
reported speech	Past Tense (e.g. were)	Past Perfect (e.g. had been)	Past Perfect (e.g. had been)	Future in the Past (e.g. would be)

<u>Would</u>, <u>could</u>, <u>might</u>, <u>should</u>, <u>ought</u> <u>to</u> remain unchanged.

Exercise 1: Reported Speech

Write down what the doctor said to Mrs Greene and what she said after the operation.

Doctor: "You need an operation. It's very simple. An operation is really necessary."
"It won't be painful. The operation will help your eyes. Your eyes will be much better."

Mrs G.: "The operation was not painful. The headaches stopped immediately. And the pills helped too."

Exercise 2: Mrs Greene and her boss

Reported Speech. Fill in the gaps.

Last week Mrs Greene asked her boss for a holiday. She did not tell him that she ... (have) problems with her eyes and that she ... (have) to have an operation. Her boss said that he ... (be) sorry but it ... (not – be) possible.
Mrs Greene told her family that she ... (cannot – have) time off and that she ... (not – have) the operation. Her son then said that he ... (go and talk) to his mother's boss and that he ... (explain) about the operation.

Exercise 3: A report

Imagine somebody has told you about an interesting experience or event. Using reported speech, retell this.

Conditional Clauses

Type 1: a) general condition (what happens always or regularly)
If the door **is** open, I **can go** out.
(if-clause and main clause: Present Tense)
b) open future condition (the condition may be fulfilled)
If I **see** a burglar in our house, I **will phone** the police.
(if-clause: Present Tense main clause: Future Tense)

Type 2: The condition cannot be fulfilled
If I **saw** a burglar in our house, I **would phone** the police.
(if-clause: Past Tense main clause: Conditional)

Type 3: Unfulfilled condition in the past
If I **had seen** a burglar in the house, I **would have phoned** the police.
(if-clause: Past Perfect main clause: Conditional Perfect)

Exercise 1: Going to a meeting in London

get up at 7	get an early train
catch the early train	get to the meeting in time
leave here too late	be late for the meeting
read the instructions	find the meeting place easily
read the papers sent to me	be well prepared for the meeting
be well prepared	follow the discussion easily
know what to say	negotiate successfully
be successful	be satisfied with the meeting

Write sentences using the expressions from the table above.

1) What will you do if you go to the meeting?
2) What would you do if you went to the meeting?
3) What would you have done if you had gone to the meeting?

Exercise 2: Speculate!

Write conditional sentences using the information from the texts you have read.

Example:
Miriam – not be so different > If Miriam was (were) not so different Karin and Julie would not play tricks on her.

1. From: *Locker 160*

lockers	in the school ...
somebody	observe Julie and Karin ...
headmaster	be told about what ...
Miriam	tell her mother about the tricks ...

2. From: *The Big Race*

Gordon's father	be not that ambitious ...
Gordon's father	treat his son more gently ...
the boy	not let Gordon win ...

3. From: *Manhood*

Mr Willison	be not so ambitious …
Mr Willison	not take Rob on such a long bike ride …
Rob	be a little stronger …
Mr Willison	not give Rob a punch ball …
Rob	not so obedient …
Mr Willison	know that there not be a boxing team at Rob's school …

4. From: *Jumping*

Jerry	not meet Denise …
Denise	not talk to Jerry …
Jerry	jump from the bridge …

5. From: *Boston: Today and Yesterday*

you	go to Boston …
you	go to the Bull & Finch Pub …
alcohol breath test	not introduce at Duxbury High School …